ESTHER

THE OLD TESTAMENT LIBRARY

Editorial Advisory Board

Jon D. Levenson

ESTHER

A Commentary

 Westminster John Knox Press
Louisville, Kentucky

Book design by Jennifer K. Cox

First edition

Published by Westminster John Knox Press
Louisville, Kentucky

This book is printed on acid-free paper that meets the American National Standards Institute Z39.48 standard.♾

PRINTED IN THE UNITED STATES OF AMERICA

97 98 99 00 01 02 03 04 05 06 — 10 9 8 7 6 5 4 3 2 1

Library of Congress Cataloging-in-Publication Data

Levenson, Jon Douglas.
    Esther : a commentary / Jon D. Levenson.—1st ed.
        p.   cm. — (Old Testament library)
    Includes bibliographical references and indexes.
    ISBN 0-664-22093-2 (alk. paper)
    1. Bible. O.T. Esther—Commentaries. I. Title. II. Series.
BS1375. 3. L48   1997
222′ . 9077—dc20   96-43247

In Memoriam

Ruth Miriam Levenson

Proverbs 31:12

CONTENTS

ESTHER

PREFACE

The excellent work of three individuals aided me enormously in the composition of this commentary. My research assistant and teaching fellow, Larry L. Lyke, performed the thankless tasks of procuring library materials for me, checking all scriptural and kindred citations, and proofreading various drafts of the manuscript. I have also profited from many conversations with him about the literary dimension of the book of Esther. My secretary, Brian D. Murphy, performed his typing with his accustomed rapidity and accuracy and often exceeded the call of duty. Finally, another of my research assistants and teaching fellows, Michelle Kwitkin, helped with the proofs and saved me from several unconscionable errors.

I also owe thanks to three individuals who served as editors at Westminster John Knox Press during the years in which I was at work on this project: Cynthia Thompson, who first recruited me for it, Jeffries Hamilton, who first worked with me on it, and Jon Berquist, who saw the volume through to production.

Much of the writing was done during my sabbatical from Harvard Divinity School in the fall semester of 1995–96. I am grateful to the school for the support I received during that semester.

Biblical references follow the Hebrew enumeration.

ABBREVIATIONS

AB	Anchor Bible
ABD	*Anchor Bible Dictionary*
AJSL	*American Journal of Semitic Languages*
Ant.	Josephus, *Jewish Antiquities*
AT	Alpha Text
b.	*Babylonian Talmud*
BA	*Biblical Archaeologist*
BHS	*Biblia Hebraica Stuttgartensia*
BKAT	Biblischer Kommentar, Altes Testament
CBQ	*Catholic Biblical Quarterly*
DSD	*Dead Sea Discoveries*
ET	*Expository Times*
FCB	Feminist Companion to the Bible
HAT	Handbuch zum Alten Testament
HDR	Harvard Dissertations in Religion
HTR	*Harvard Theological Review*
HUCA	*Hebrew Union College Annual*
ICC	International Critical Commentary
JBL	*Journal of Biblical Literature*
JES	*Journal of Ecumenical Studies*
JQR	*Jewish Quarterly Review*
JR	*Journal of Religion*
JSOT	*Journal for the Study of the Old Testament*
JSOTSup	Journal for the Study of the Old Testament Supplement Series
JTS	*Journal of Theological Studies*
KAT	Kommentar zum Alten Testament
LB	*Linguistica Biblica*
LCBI	Literary Currents in Biblical Interpretation
LCL	Loeb Classical Library
LXX	Septuagint
Meg.	Tractate *Megillah*
MT	Masoretic Text

OBT	Overtures to Biblical Theology
OL	Old Latin
OTL	Old Testament Library
PRK	*Pesiqta de-Rab Kahana*
RHA	*Revue Hittite et Asianique*
RQ	*Revue de Qumrân*
SBLDS	Society of Biblical Literature Dissertation Series
SBLMS	Society of Biblical Literature Monograph Series
SBM	Stuttgarter biblische Monographien
Ta'an.	Tractate *Ta'anit*
TEH	Theologische Existenz heute
TZ	*Theologische Zeitschrift*
USQR	*Union Seminary Quarterly Review*
VT	*Vetus Testamentum*
Yeb.	Tractate *Yebamot*
ZAW	*Zeitschrift für die alttestamentliche Wissenschaft*

SELECT BIBLIOGRAPHY

Ackroyd, Peter R. *Exile and Restoration,* OTL, Philadelphia, 1968.

Alter, Robert, and Frank Kermode. *The Literary Guide to the Bible,* Cambridge, Mass., 1987.

Anderson, Bernhard W. "The Place of the Book of Esther in the Christian Bible," *JR* 30 (1950): 32–43.

Ashkenazi, Eliezer. *Yosef Leqah,* in *Megillat Esther 'im Perush Ha-Gr"a Ha-Shalem* [Elijah, Gaon of Vilna], ed. Chanan David Nobel, Jerusalem, 5752/1991.

Bardtke, Hans. *Das Buch Esther,* KAT 17:5, Gütersloh, 1963.

Berg, Sandra Beth. *The Book of Esther,* SBLDS 44, Missoula, Mont.,1979.

Bergey, Ronald L. "Late Linguistic Features in Esther," *JQR* 75 (1984): 66–78.

Berquist, Jon L. *Judaism in Persia's Shadow,* Minneapolis, 1995.

Bickerman, Elias. "The Colophon of the Greek Book of Esther," *JBL* 63 (1944): 339–62.

―――. *Four Strange Books of the Bible,* New York, 1967.

Brenner, Athalya. "Looking at Esther through the Looking Glass," *A Feminist Companion to Esther, Judith and Susanna,* ed. Athalya Brenner, FCB 7, Sheffield, 1991, 71–80.

Bronner, Leila Leah. "Esther Revisited: An Aggadic Approach," *A Feminist Companion to Esther, Judith and Susanna,* ed. Athalya Brenner, FCB 7, Sheffield, 1991, 176–97.

Cazelles, Henri. "Note sur la composition du rouleau d'Esther," *Lex tua veritas: Festschrift für Hubert Junker,* ed. H. Gross and F. Mussner, Trier, 1961, 17–29.

Clines, David J. A. *The Esther Scroll,* JSOTSup 30, Sheffield, 1984.

Cohen, Abraham D. " 'Hu Ha-goral': The Religious Significance of Esther," *Judaism* 23 (1974): 87–94.

Collins, John J. "The Court-Tales in Daniel and the Development of Apocalyptic," *JBL* 94 (1975): 218–34.

Craig, Kenneth. *Reading Esther: A Case for the Literary Carnivalesque,* LCBI, Louisville, Ky., 1995.

Crenshaw, James L. "Method in Determining Wisdom Influence upon 'Historical' Literature," *JBL* 88 (1969): 129–42.

Daube, David. "The Last Chapter of Esther," *JQR* 37 (1946–47): 139–47.

Dommershausen, Werner. *Die Estherrolle,* SBM 6, Stuttgart, 1968.

Duchesne-Guillemin, Jacques. "Les noms des eunuques d'Assuérus," *Muséon* 66 (1953): 105–108.

Ehrlich, Arnold B. *Randglossen zur hebräischen Bibel,* Leipzig, 1914.

Fox, Michael V. *Character and Ideology in the Book of Esther,* Columbia, S.C., 1991.

———. *The Redaction of the Books of Esther,* SBLMS 40, Atlanta, 1991.

Gan, Moshe. "The Book of Esther in the Light of the Story of Joseph in Egypt" (Hebrew), *Tarbiz* 31 (1961–62): 144–49.

Gaster, Theodor H. *Purim and Hanukkah in Custom and Tradition,* New York, 1950.

Gehman, Henry S. "Notes on the Persian Words in the Book of Esther," *JBL* 43 (1924): 321–28.

Gerleman, Gillis. *Esther,* BKAT 21, Neukirchen-Vluyn, 1982.

Goldman, Stan. "Narrative and Ethical Ironies in Esther," *JSOT* 47 (1990): 15–31.

Gordis, Robert. "Studies in the Esther Narrative," *JBL* 95 (1976): 43–58.

Greenstein, Edward L. "A Jewish Reading of Esther," *Judaic Perspectives on Ancient Israel,* ed. J. Neusner et al., Philadelphia, 1987, 225–43.

Grossfeld, Bernard. *The Two Esther Targums,* New York, 1991.

Hakham, Amos. *Esther,* in *The Five Scrolls, Da'at Hammiqra'* (Hebrew), Jerusalem, 1973.

Haupt, Paul. "Critical Notes on Esther," *AJSL* 24 (1908): 97–186.

———. *Purim,* Baltimore and Leipzig, 1906.

Hengel, Martin. *Judaism and Hellenism,* 2 vols., Philadelphia, 1974.

Herodotus. *History,* 4 vols., LCL, Cambridge, Mass., and London, 1981–82.

Herst, Roger E. "The Purim Connection," *USQR* 28 (1973): 139–45.

Humphreys, W. Lee. "A Life-Style for Diaspora: A Study of the Tales of Esther and Daniel," *JBL* 92 (1973): 211–23.

Ibn Ezra, Abraham, commentary on Esther, in the traditional Rabbinic Bible (*Miqra'ot Gedolot*).

Jones, Bruce William. "Two Misconceptions about the Book of Esther," *CBQ* 39 (1977): 171–81.

Klein, Lillian. "Honor and Shame in Esther," *A Feminist Companion to Esther, Judith and Susanna,* ed. Athalya Brenner, FCB 7, Sheffield, 1991, 149–75.

LaCocque, André. *The Feminine Unconventional: Four Subversive Figures in Israel's Tradition,* OBT, Minneapolis, 1990.

Lebram, J.C.H. "Purimfest und Estherbuch," *VT* 22 (1972): 208–22.

Levenson, Jon D. "The Scroll of Esther in Ecumenical Perspective," *JES* 13 (1976): 440–51.

Lewy, J. "The Feast of the 14th Day of Adar," *HUCA* 14 (1939): 127–51.

———. "Old Assyrian *puru'um* and *pūrum,*" *RHA* 36 (1938): 117–24.

Loader, J. A. "Esther as a Novel with Different Levels of Meaning," *ZAW* 90 (1978): 417–21.

Loewenstamm, Samuel E. "Esther 9:29–32: The Genesis of a Late Addition," *HUCA* 42 (1971): 117–24.

Mayer, Rudolf. "Iranischer Beitrag zu Problemen des Daniel und Esther-Buches," *Lex tua veritas: Festschrift für Hubert Junker*, ed. H. Gross and F. Mussner, Trier, 1961, 127–35.

McKane, W. "A Note on Esther IX and I Samuel XV," *JTS* 12 (1961): 260–61.

Meinhold, Arndt. "Die Gattung der Josephgeschichte und des Estherbuches: Diasporanovelle I & II," *ZAW* 87 (1975): 306–24; 88 (1976): 79–93.

———. "Theologische Erwägungen zum Buch Esther," *TZ* 34 (1978): 321–33.

Meyers, Carol. *Discovering Eve: Ancient Israelite Women in Context,* London and New York, 1988.

Milik, J. T. "Les Modèles araméens du livre d'Esther dans la grotte 4 de Qumrân," *RQ* 15 (1992): 321–99 and plates I–VII.

Moore, Carey A. "Archaeology and the Book of Esther," *BA* 38 (1975): 62–79.

———. *Daniel, Esther, and Jeremiah: The Additions,* AB 44, Garden City, N.Y., 1977.

———. *Esther,* AB 7B, Garden City, N.Y., 1971.

———. "Esther, Book of," *Anchor Bible Dictionary,* vol. 2, ed. David Noel Freedman, New York, 1992, 633–43.

———. "Esther Revisited: An Examination of Esther Studies over the Past Decade," *Biblical Studies in Honor of Samuel Iwry,* ed. A. Kort and S. Morschauser, Winona Lake, Ind., 1985, 163–72.

———. "A Greek Witness to a Different Hebrew Text of Esther," *ZAW* 79 (1967): 351–58.

———. *Studies in the Book of Esther,* Library of Biblical Studies, New York, 1982.

Morris, A. E. "The Purpose of the Book of Esther," *ET* 42 (1930–31): 124–28.

Naveh, Joseph, and Jonas C. Greenfield. "Hebrew and Aramaic in the Persian Period," *The Cambridge History of Judaism,* ed. W. D. Davies and L. Finkelstein, vol. 1, *Introduction: The Persian Period,* Cambridge, 1984, 115–29.

Niditch, Susan. "Legends of Wise Heroes and Heroines," *The Hebrew Bible and Its Modern Interpreters,* ed. Douglas A. Knight and Gene M. Tucker, Philadelphia/Chico, Calif., 1985, 445–63.

———. *Underdogs and Tricksters,* San Francisco, 1987.

Niditch, Susan, and Robert Doran. "The Success Story of the Wise Courtier: A Formal Approach," *JBL* 96 (1977): 179–93.

Olmstead, A. T. *The History of the Persian Empire,* Chicago, 1948.

Paton, Lewis B. *A Critical and Exegetical Commentary on the Book of Esther*, ICC, Edinburgh, 1908.

Radday, Yehuda T. "Chiasm in Joshua, Judges and Others," *LB* 27/28 (1973): 6–13.

Rashi (Rabbi Shlomo Yitschaqi), commentary on Esther, in the traditional Rabbinic Bible (*Miqra'ot Gedolot*).

Rosenthal, Ludwig A. "Die Josephsgeschichte mit den Büchern Ester und Daniel verglichen," *ZAW* 15 (1895): 278–84.

Sasson, Jack M. "Esther," *The Literary Guide to the Bible*, ed. Robert Alter and Frank Kermode, Cambridge, Mass., 1987, 335–42.

Schauss, Hayyim. *The Jewish Festivals*, trans. Samuel Jaffe, Cincinnati, 1938.

Talmon, Shemaryahu. " 'Wisdom' in the Book of Esther," *VT* 13 (1963): 419–55; rpt., *Literary Studies in the Hebrew Bible*, Jerusalem and Leiden, 1993, 255–90.

———. "Was the Book of Esther Known at Qumran?" *DSD* 2 (1995): 249–67.

Tcherikover, Victor. *Hellenistic Civilization and the Jews*, Philadelphia, 1959.

Torrey, Charles C. "The Older Book of Esther," *HTR* 37 (1944): 1–40.

Vischer, Wilhelm. *Esther*, TEH 48, Munich, 1937.

Walfish, Barry Dov. *Esther in Medieval Garb: Jewish Interpretation of the Book of Esther in the Middle Ages*, SUNY Series in Judaica, Albany, N.Y., 1993.

White, Sidnie Ann. "Esther," *The Women's Bible Commentary*, ed. Carol A. Newsom and Sharon H. Ringe, Louisville, Ky., 1992, 124–29.

———. "Esther: A Feminine Model for Jewish Diaspora," *Gender and Difference in Ancient Israel*, ed. Peggy L. Day, Minneapolis, 1989, 161–77.

Wills, Lawrence M. *The Jew in the Court of the Foreign King*, HDR, Minneapolis, 1990.

Würthwein, Ernst. *Die fünf Megilloth*, HAT 18, Tübingen, 1969.

Xenophon. *Anabasis*, LCL, London/New York/Cambridge, Mass., 1922.

INTRODUCTION

The book of Esther is many things, so many, in fact, that it would be a capital mistake to view it from only one angle. It is, for example, a tale of intrigue at court, a story of lethal danger to the Jews narrowly averted by heroic rescue. It is also a tale of the ascent of an orphan in exile to the rank of the most powerful woman—and perhaps even the most powerful person—in the empire and, arguably, the world. The book of Esther is the story of how a humiliated and endangered minority, the Jews of the eastern Diaspora after the Babylonian exile, came to be respected and feared by the Gentile majority and to see one of their own honored by appointment to the second highest post in the empire. It is the comical story of a pompous fool who does himself in and the chilling tale of the narrow escape from death of a despised and ever-vulnerable minority. It is all these things and more, and readers who are satisfied that they know what Esther means would be well advised to examine it again in search of other dimensions. For the author of this commentary affirms without reservation that a few years of close textual work on the book and involvement in scholarship on it have immeasurably enriched his reading of it and proven it in his mind to be a vastly more complex piece of literature than he had previously thought.

Full of action, with few and perhaps no scenes that could be omitted without damage, the book relies more on narration and less on quoted speech than most comparable biblical material. Indeed, the direct address of one of its heroes, Mordecai, is limited to two verses (4:13–14), although this speech, like most of those in Esther, is fraught with importance and marks a key turning point in the narrative. In order to understand the overall design of the book and how its author conveys its multiple messages, we must first summarize the action.

1. The Plot of the Book of Esther

The book of Esther begins when Ahasuerus, king of the Persians and the Medes, gives two exceedingly lavish banquets: the first for the elite of his entire empire and the second for the men of the fortified compound of his capital, Susa (1:1–8). In addition, his consort, Queen Vashti, gives a banquet, the third mentioned so far, for the women of the royal palace (v. 9). Things quickly turn ugly, however, when the queen, defying her intoxicated husband, disobeys his summons to appear at his banquet so that he might show off her beauty to the assembled company. This sends him into an uncontrollable but not uncharacteristic rage. The queen's insubordination provokes a state crisis, as the king consults his seven trusted councillors as to how to proceed (vv. 13–15). The result is a further escalation of the crisis, for the domestic difficulties of the royal couple become the occasion for an imperial edict deposing Vashti and ordering every man to be master of his household, a task at which the king who issues the edict has proven a conspicuous failure (vv. 16–22).

Some time later, celibacy not being Ahasuerus's forte, he orders every beautiful young virgin throughout his vast empire to appear in his compound and be given the appropriate cosmetics in preparation for a competition for the position of queen (2:1–4). Among the maidens of the capital city is a gorgeous Jewess with the Hebrew name Hadassah, though known throughout the rest of the tale by her Gentile name, Esther. She is not only an exile but an orphan as well, having been adopted by her cousin Mordecai, who seems to be a courtier and whose genealogy suggests a connection to the ancient king of Israel, Saul (vv. 5–7). Disguising her ethnicity on her foster father's orders, Esther enters the contest, mysteriously wins the favor of the harem-keeper and, less mysteriously, wins the king's favor as well and becomes the queen. This is the occasion of the fourth banquet of the tale, celebrating the enthronement of the new consort (vv. 8–20).

Then, in a vignette that seems unrelated but proves crucial to the denouement, Mordecai learns of an assassination plotted by two courtiers and, through the intervention of Esther, alerts the king and thus saves his life (vv. 21–23).

What follows, however, is not the king's rewarding Mordecai, delayed until chap. 6, but his promotion to prime minister of one Haman, whose ancestry suggests a connection to King Agag of the Amalekites (whom Saul inexcusably spared, thus dooming his own kingship). For reasons the text never specifies, Mordecai refuses to bow before the new prime minister. Haman retaliates by resolving to annihilate all the Jews in Ahasuerus's empire (3:1–6). He casts a lot (*pûr*) to determine the auspicious day for the mass murder, and — accusing the Jews of being different and insubordinate to the king and offering an enormous bribe — he easily wins Ahasuerus's consent (vv. 7–11). An edict is issued instructing the populace to destroy all the Jews, including women and children, eleven months hence, on the thirteenth of Adar. While the city of Susa is thrown into pandemonium, the king and Haman sit down to yet another banquet, the fifth in the book of Esther (vv. 12–15).

Having learned of the decree of genocide, the Jews in general and Mordecai in particular engage in public rites of mourning, causing Queen Esther to be greatly upset. In protracted discussion through an intermediary, Mordecai attempts to persuade his cousin to intercede with the king, but she, doubtless mindful of Vashti's fate, will not defy the rule that no one may approach the king un-summoned (4:1–11). To this Mordecai rejoins that if Esther, who may have risen to queenship for this very moment, remains silent, deliverance will still come to them from some mysterious other quarter, but she and her close kin will perish. His eloquence induces her to accept her fate, and, calling upon Mordecai to organize a three-day fast in support of her, she resolves to take the risk of approaching the king in hopes of averting the annihilation of her race (vv. 12–16).

When the fateful day arrives, the king, ever malleable and amenable, grants Esther whatever she wishes, but she, in turn, asks only for a banquet, the sixth in the book, for the royal couple and Haman. At the banquet itself, again offered whatever she wishes, Esther requests only another banquet of the same threesome (5:1–8). This sends Haman into ecstasy—until, that is, he again encounters Mordecai, who continues to refuse him homage. Predictably enraged, the prime minister boasts to his friends and his wife about his high status and great wealth to make the point that it is all meaningless as long as Mordecai is free to enter his field of vision. Haman's wife and friends then make a suggestion that he, the architect of the empire-wide plan of genocide, had oddly never considered: to have the Jew Mordecai himself impaled upon a giant stake. Like Ahasuerus at his state council, Haman immediately accepts (vv. 9–14).

In the next scene, perhaps the funniest of the book, we find the king treating his insomnia by having the royal annals read to him. It so happens that the passage he hears tells of the assassination attempt that Mordecai had foiled. The king, resolved to recompense his benefactor, asks the only courtier of rank in attendance what should be done to reward a good deed. That courtier turns out to be none other than Haman, who was just then coming in to ask for permission to impale his nemesis, the king's benefactor. Unable to imagine that the king would wish to honor anyone more than him, Haman suggests that the honoree be treated as a kind of substitute king,[1] allowed to wear royal garb and to ride the king's horse. The king agrees and orders Haman to put his plans into effect, only it is Mordecai who will benefit and Haman who will serve as his archenemy's herald in the procession he devised. Humiliated, and (like Mordecai in chap. 4) in mourning as well, Haman hurries home to his friends and his wife, who now have a different and more ominous message for him: If Mordecai is Jewish, Haman will never overcome him but will only fall before him (6:1–14).

At the climactic second banquet of Esther, Ahasuerus, and Haman—the seventh banquet of the book—Esther at last, with great eloquence, makes her plaintive appeal. The king, ostensibly oblivious to his own involvement in the great conspiracy, demands to know who had the nerve to devise it. When

[1]Jack Sasson, "Esther," in *The Literary Guide to the Bible,* ed. Robert Alter and Frank Kermode, Cambridge, Mass., 1987, 341. See Simo Parpola, *Letters from Assyrian Scholars to the Kings Esarhaddon and Assurbanipal,* Kevelaer and Neukirchen-Vluyn, 1983, 2:xxii–xxxii, esp. xxix, on Her. 7:15, 17.

Esther names Haman, the king exits in another rage, and Haman falls onto Esther's couch to plead for his own life (7:1–7). Returning, again at just the right moment, the king utters the funniest line of the whole book: "Does he also intend to violate the queen while I am in the palace?" (7:8). A eunuch, Harbona, then has to intervene to suggest the obvious resolution: to impale the queen's enemy Haman on the giant stake that he erected for the king's benefactor Mordecai. Haman is hoist with his own petard (7:1–10).

The king awards Haman's estate to Esther. Her husband having finally gotten straight who is his enemy and who is his friend, Esther ushers Mordecai into Ahasuerus's presence, and the king promotes Mordecai into Haman's position. Still the problem of the irrevocable edict of genocide remains, and despite another moving and eloquent plea from the queen, Ahasuerus cannot withdraw it. Instead, he can only authorize Esther and Mordecai to draw up their own counter-decree (8:1–8). Thus, two months and ten days after Ahasuerus ordered the liquidation of the Jews, a second edict goes forth authorizing the Jews throughout the empire to assemble in self-defense and retaliation against the anti-Semites on the very day that Haman had chosen by lot for the Jews to be eliminated (vv. 9–14).

Mordecai emerges from his audience with the king cloaked again in royal garb, only this time indefinitely rather than temporarily. The Jews are ecstatic at his ascent and the chance to defend themselves, and they celebrate with the eighth banquet of the book of Esther. Many Gentiles identify themselves with the Jews in some fashion or another, for the once despised nation now inspires fear (vv. 15–17).

When the fateful day arrives, the reverse of what had been planned occurs, for the Jews overwhelm their enemies, the royal officials aiding them out of fear of Mordecai. Haman's ten sons are killed and, at Esther's request, impaled as a sign of public disgrace, but no spoil is taken. In Susa itself, the Jews reassemble on the fourteenth of Adar and rest on the fifteenth, thus setting a precedent for the celebration of the new holiday of Purim (after *pûr,* the lot that Haman cast), celebrated on the fifteenth for residents of large cities as opposed to the fourteenth for all other Jews. These two days of feasting comprise the ninth and tenth feasts of the book of Esther (9:1–19).

Mordecai and Esther, both individually and jointly, issue encyclicals enjoining the celebration of Purim upon the Jews, their descendants, and converts to Judaism for all time. The manner of its observance is to be defined by joyous banqueting and the giving of gifts to each other and to the poor. The Jewish community irrevocably accepts to observe Purim in the manner Mordecai and Esther have prescribed (vv. 20–32).

The book of Esther closes with a brief annalistic note about Ahasuerus's success and the high position of Mordecai, second-in-command to the king and a self-identified Jew who continually pursued the welfare of his people (10:1–3).

2. Structure and Style

The fast pace of the action in the book of Esther can mask the substantial elements of symmetry in its narrative design. One central structuring element is the sequence of banquets throughout the book, as indicated on the left side of figure 1, adapted from Michael V. Fox.[2]

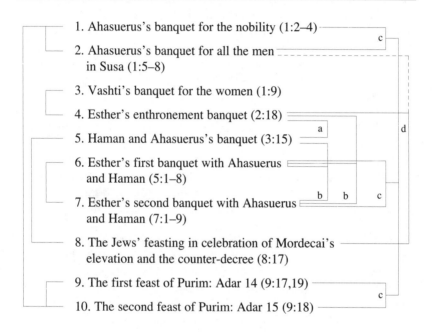

1. Ahasuerus's banquet for the nobility (1:2–4)

2. Ahasuerus's banquet for all the men in Susa (1:5–8)

3. Vashti's banquet for the women (1:9)

4. Esther's enthronement banquet (2:18)

5. Haman and Ahasuerus's banquet (3:15)

6. Esther's first banquet with Ahasuerus and Haman (5:1–8)

7. Esther's second banquet with Ahasuerus and Haman (7:1–9)

8. The Jews' feasting in celebration of Mordecai's elevation and the counter-decree (8:17)

9. The first feast of Purim: Adar 14 (9:17,19)

10. The second feast of Purim: Adar 15 (9:18)

FIGURE 1

The correspondence of the first two banquets with the last two gives the book of Esther in its surviving Hebrew form a kind of envelope structure. The action ends (more or less) where it begins, with two banquets, the first in each case for residents of the entire empire and the second for those in the capital, Susa. Vashti's banquet and Esther's (nos. 3 and 4) are both parallel and contrastive. Both are certainly in honor of a beautiful queen and possibly in celebration of a wedding (see the commentary on 1:1–9). But Vashti's is her last banquet, and Esther's, her first. Fox's helpful chart correctly notes the contrast of banquets 5 and 8: The first celebrates Haman's successful passage of his

[2]Michael V. Fox, *Character and Ideology in the Book of Esther,* Studies on Personalities of the Old Testament, Columbia, S.C., 1991, 157.

death sentence against the Jews, and the second is the Jews' celebration of
Mordecai's elevation to prime minister in place of Haman and the successful
passage of the counter-decree. But, as noted by the lines on the right-hand side
(which I have added to Fox's chart), banquets 4 and 5 are also to be paired (a);
each is the first of three for the central figure (Esther and Haman, respectively)
with Ahasuerus (b). The two banquets for the threesome (nos. 6 and 7) are obviously to be paired, and it is possible that they reflect the opening and closing
pairs (nos. 1–2 and 9–10) as well: In each set, the first banquet (nos. 1, 6, and
9) is more general and less conclusive, and the second (nos. 2, 7, and 10) is
more focused and climactic. Banquet 2 thus results in the deposition of Queen
Vashti, no. 7 in the execution of Prime Minister Haman, and no. 10 celebrates
the final elimination of the murderous anti-Semites from the body politic. In
addition, banquet 8, which celebrates Mordecai's emergence from the palace
with a huge golden diadem on his head, has affinities with no. 4, which celebrates Esther's coronation, and, more distantly, with banquet 2, in which the
crisis develops when Ahasuerus orders Vashti to appear in her royal diadem
(c) (1:11).

In summary, one way to view the structure of the narrative is in terms of its
ten banquets—that is, five sets of two—though there are elaborate correspon-
dences between banquets that are not immediately paired, and the correspon-
dences even within pairs are both synthetic and antithetic. All this is hardly surprising, since the practical objective of the book of Esther in its surviving
Hebrew form is to authorize and regulate the Feast of Purim, which in the aggregate is a two-day celebration marked by festive banqueting. An analogy
with Gen. 1:1–2:3, the opening creation story of the Pentateuch, suggests itself. The prime practical objective of that passage is to authorize the observance of a day of rest every seven days, but the strings of seven items within
the verses include far more than the schema of seven days of creation, and only
close examination reveals them.[3]

It should be noted that the counterpoint to banqueting is fasting. Thus, the
report of banquet 5, of Ahasuerus and Haman, is followed immediately by a
report of Mordecai and the other Jews' public rites of lamentation and mourning, of which fasting, explicitly mentioned, is an important element (4:1–3).
Similarly, Esther initiates a three-day fast just before asking the king for
the two banquets that culminate in Haman's destruction (vv. 16–17). Between
those two banquets is found the scene of the royal procession, after which
it is Haman whom we now see in mourning (6:12), but only briefly. For
like Esther's, his mourning precedes a banquet to which he is whisked off (v.
14). The reversals in the book of Esther are so frequent, and the suspense so
high, that it can be misleading to speak of any given scene as the pivotal mo-

---

[3]See Jon D. Levenson, *Creation and the Persistence of Evil*, San Francisco, 1988, 66–68.

ment of its plot. But chap. 6 surely defines the pivotal moment, for the royal procession foreshadows the reversal of Mordecai and Haman, as the former sheds his sackcloth and ashes for royal garb, and the latter hurries home in mourning. Note that this occurs between Esther's two banquets with Haman and the king (nos. 6 and 7), a point that 6:14 nicely underscores. This abrupt alternation of self-affliction and self-indulgence comes to self-conscious expression in the last letters of Esther and Mordecai dispatched "in order to make these days of Purim obligatory in their appointed times, just as Mordecai the Jew and Queen Esther had prescribed and just as [the Jews] had accepted for themselves and their descendants the obligation of fasts and lamentation" (9:31).

Lest we imagine that the reversal of status between Mordecai and Haman, the pivotal sixth chapter, is only a passing phenomenon, the latter's advisers and his wife, Zeresh, provide an interpretation suggesting that higher forces are at work: "If Mordecai, before whom you have begun to fall, is of Jewish descent, you will never overcome him. You shall collapse altogether before him" (v. 13). To be sure, much suspense remains, for this scene is the pivot but not the climax, and we cannot yet be altogether sure that Ahasuerus will respond positively to Esther at the second banquet of the threesome; or that he will be willing to oppose his hand-picked prime minister and the anti-Jewish edict that he personally authorized; or that, these things having been done, the Jews will prevail in the melee that ensues on the thirteenth of Adar. In short, the suspense may slacken a bit once the royal procession has foreshadowed the great reversal, but neither modern readers nor the Jews about whom they are reading can rest content until the action is concluded in chap. 9.

Our identification of chap. 6 as the pivot offers another angle of vision on the structure of the book of Esther. Whereas the ten banquets serve to highlight the changes in fortune that are a key motif of the entire tale, the identification of the pivotal scene uncovers a larger pattern of symmetry that can best be conveyed in figure 2. The symmetry is not perfect, of course, as it seldom is in great works of literature. For example, the fateful exchange of Ahasuerus and Esther in which Haman is exposed (F') occurs *during* the second banquet of the powerful threesome (G'), so that 7:1–6 corresponds to both F and G. Similarly, though the greatness of Ahasuerus (*gĕdûllâ*, 1:4) with which the book opens (A) corresponds to the account of the vast range of his power and the greatness (*gādôl*, 10:3) of his new prime minister, Mordecai the Jew, with which it closes (A'), it is also the case that the opening scene is a banquet and thus corresponds as well to the first banquet of Purim, that is, to the celebration by village Jews on the fourteenth of Adar (9:17, 19 in B'). Despite the imperfections of the symmetry and the existence of elements that have no close parallel on the other side of the V-shaped figure (e.g., the ascent of Esther [2:17] and the foiling of the assassination conspiracy [vv. 21–23]), our

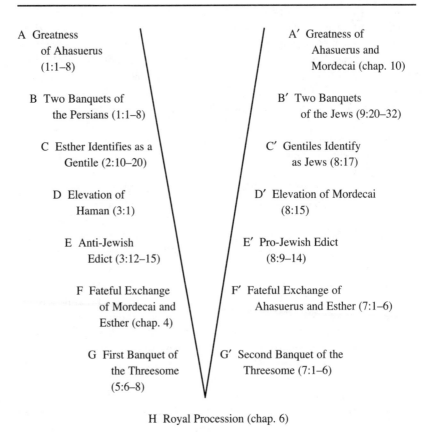

A Greatness
    of Ahasuerus
    (1:1–8)

  B Two Banquets of
      the Persians (1:1–8)

    C Esther Identifies as a
        Gentile (2:10–20)

      D Elevation of
          Haman (3:1)

        E Anti-Jewish
            Edict (3:12–15)

          F Fateful Exchange
              of Mordecai and
              Esther (chap. 4)

            G First Banquet of
                the Threesome
                (5:6–8)

A′ Greatness of
    Ahasuerus and
    Mordecai (chap. 10)

  B′ Two Banquets
      of the Jews (9:20–32)

    C′ Gentiles Identify
        as Jews (8:17)

      D′ Elevation of Mordecai
          (8:15)

        E′ Pro-Jewish Edict
            (8:9–14)

          F′ Fateful Exchange of
              Ahasuerus and Esther (7:1–6)

           G′ Second Banquet of the
               Threesome (7:1–6)

H Royal Procession (chap. 6)

FIGURE 2

diagram places it beyond doubt that in its largest design the book displays a bilateral chiastic structure,[4] in which the events in the first half (A–G) have at best an inconclusive and, more often, a negative cast, whereas those in the second half (G′–A′) are uniformly positive and usually correct the deficiencies of their counterparts. As a student stated in a seminar,[5] the theme of the entire book is summed up in two Hebrew words—*nahăpôk hû'*, "the reverse occurred" (9:1). The very structure of Esther suggests the transformation "from

---

[4]See Yehuda T. Radday, "Chiasm in Joshua, Judges, and Others," *LB* 27/28 (Sept. 1973): 9–10, and Sandra Beth Berg, *The Book of Esther,* SBLDS 44, Missoula, Mont., 1979, 106–13.

[5]Brooks Schramm, in "Esther and Its Jewish Exegesis," seminar at the University of Chicago Divinity School, Winter 1986.

a time of grief to one of joy, and from an occasion of mourning to a holiday" (v. 22), which is its great theme.

Even in the case of passages that our V-shaped diagram cannot accommodate, there are meaningful elements of symmetry and narrative analogy. Consider for the sake of example the parallels between Vashti's and Mordecai's refusals to comply with the king's command. Vashti's refusal to attend the party (1:10–12) results in a session of the king's council that offers a proposal that she be banished and perhaps killed as well (vv. 13–20), which the king accepts (vv. 21–22). Similarly, Mordecai's refusal to prostrate himself before Haman (3:1–4)—also a violation of a royal command (v. 3)—results in a meeting of the prime minister and the king and a proposal that the Jews be eliminated (vv. 8–9), which the king again accepts (vv. 10–11). In the case of this point of symmetry, the structure is linear rather than chiastic; the events are in the same order and not in reverse, as they would be if they were on the opposing wings of our V-shaped figure. This direct parallel also serves a larger literary purpose, however, for it enhances the readers' expectation that Mordecai will share Vashti's fate, but—*nahăpôk hû'*—the reverse occurs: He is publicly honored and promoted (chap. 6; 8:15), whereas she is disgraced and banished (1:16–22). In fact, Mordecai's public parade in royal garb corresponds in one sense to the requested public display of Vashti "wearing a royal diadem" (1:11) that never took place and that led to her banishment. Yet in other senses the two events are opposite: For example, Vashti was to be displayed for her physical attributes only and thus as an expression of the king's self-indulgence, whereas Mordecai is paraded for having saved the king's life and thus as an expression of Ahasuerus's gratitude and loyalty. Here again we find the author setting up structures that are closely parallel on the one hand, but that reveal important thematic contrasts on the other. The broad humor with which the story is conveyed must not blind us to the subtlety with which the author has interlaced elements of similarity and difference, thus keeping the readers in continual suspense and surprise. Whereas the employment of narrative pairing and the overall symmetrical structure suggest equilibrium and stasis on one level, on another level they keep the action moving until all things fall into place with the elevation of Mordecai and the elimination of the anti-Semites. *Plus la même chose, plus ça change.*

We have now examined two angles of vision on the structure of the book of Esther. The first involves the ten banquets, which serve not only as punctuation marks in the narrative but also as commentary on the fortunes of the protagonists, especially when they are contrasted with fasts and kindred rites of self-affliction. Our second angle of vision identifies the exchange of status between Haman and Mordecai in chap. 6 as the pivotal scene and develops a substantial set of parallels between key events on each side of the pivot as an indication of a loose chiastic structure to the overall narrative. Finally, we noted that even events that are not paralleled and contrasted on the other side of the pivot can function in elaborate relationships of narrative analogy that are richly productive of meaning. It is a tribute to the complexity and sophistication of the book that there are still other helpful ways to understand its elements of structure, especially on a smaller scale. Some of these are indicated in our commentary, and its readers are invited to identify others for themselves.

Doing so will be more difficult without a knowledge of Hebrew, since so much of the artistry of the book depends on its use of key words. The deployment of the verb *nāpal*, "to fall," should suffice as an illustration. It occurs four times in the book of Esther. The first is in 3:7, when Haman has the *pûr*, or lot, cast (*hippîl*) to determine the auspicious day for the annihilation of the Jews. The second time is in the crucial speech of Haman's advisers and his wife Zeresh in 6:13, wherein the verb appears three times, the last two in an ominously intensified construction: "If Mordecai, before whom you have begun to fall (*linpōl*), is of Jewish descent, you will never overcome him. You shall collapse altogether (*nāpôl tippôl*) before him." Here, Haman's humiliation at the time of his nemesis's public acclamation is interpreted as an act of falling, and the astute reader recalls not only the casting of the lot but also Mordecai's adamant refusal to "kneel and bow down" to Haman (3:2, 5). The words are different, but the posture is comparable: once again the subtle interfusion of similarity and difference. The last appearance of *nāpal* is in 7:8, when Haman does to Esther what Mordecai refused to do to him, falling (*nōpēl*) onto her couch in abject submission. Yet that very act, which in the case of Mordecai ultimately leads to his elevation, in the case of Haman leads directly to his execution. Just as his advisers and his wife predicted, he indeed falls before Mordecai, but little did they (or we) suspect that his literal gesture of falling would be before Esther, not Mordecai, and that the king's foolishness in misinterpreting the gesture would be what does Haman in.

The style in which the book of Esther is written often complements its overall structure and is essential to the way in which it conveys its multiple messages. The pairing or doubling, which we have already stressed, can be detected, for example, not only in the five sets of two banquets, in the three pairs of men and women (Ahasuerus–Vashti, Mordecai–Esther, and Haman–Zeresh),[6] and in the numerous duplications of scenes; it is also audible in an extraordinarily large number of verbal dyads embedded in the language of the text. Greenstein finds two dozen in the first chapter alone:[7] "Ahasuerus, the same Ahasuerus"; "from India to Nubia" (1:1); "his officials and his courtiers"; "Persia and Media" (vv. 3, 14, and 19); "the noblemen and the governors" (v.

[6]Note also the pair of assassins, Bigthan and Teresh, in 2:21–23.

[7]Edward L. Greenstein, "A Jewish Reading of Esther," in *Judaic Perspectives on Ancient Israel*, ed. Jacob Neusner et al., Philadelphia, 1987, 238–39.

3); "the vast wealth of his kingdom and the resplendent glory of his majesty"; "a long period, a hundred and eighty days" (v. 4); "high and low" (v. 5); "each [lit., and every] man" (v. 8); "the seven eunuchs in attendance [lit., serving]" (v. 10); "the peoples and the officers" (v. 11); "[t]he king became highly incensed, and his rage burned within him" (v. 12); "the sages learned in precedents"; "law and justice" (v. 13); "ministers . . . [those with] access to the king's presence" (v. 14); "the king and the ministers" (v. 16); "contempt and rage" (v. 18); "another woman[,] [one] more worthy" (v. 19); "the king and the ministers" (v. 21); "each and every province"; "each and every people"; and "shall be master of his household and speak the language of his people" (v. 22).

One reason for the verbal dyads is their prominence in ancient "officialese," a type of speech that the author of Esther employs to great effect. As Sasson remarks, "he frequently adopts the style of an archivist."[8] I might add, this is why the dyads are so numerous in chap. 1, which tells only of matters transacted at court and concentrates on deliberations in the king's council of sages (vv. 13–22). Greenstein is correct, nonetheless, that "the entire text of Esther abounds in verbal doublets or dyads" and "[t]hese lend a profound effect of duality to the tale."[9]

Viewed more broadly, the dyads are a subcategory of the phenomenon that Niditch considers "[t]he most distinctive feature of style in Esther . . . the extensive use of elaborate chains of synonyms, the tendency to say the same thing two, three, or four times." As examples, she adduces, among others, the lists of seven eunuchs and seven sages (1:10, 14; note that the latter names, if read in reverse order, show a suspect similarity to the former)[10] and expressions like "destroy, slay, and annihilate" (3:13; 7:4; 8:11), "fasting, weeping, wailing, and . . . sackcloth and ashes" (4:3), "light, joy, happiness, and honor" (8:16).[11] In this connection, we must not neglect the most elaborate chain of all, the list of ten sons of Haman, arranged in two sets of three and then one of four, in which, as noted in the commentary, each set starts with a name that begins with a *p*, is accented on the penultimate syllable and ends in *t(h)a'*, and then finishes with another name with the same ending (9:7–9).[12] Here, too, the motive may be to imitate an archivistic or annalistic style in order to endow a most unlikely tale with an air of historical veracity. But, at least equally and perhaps more

---

[8]Sasson, "Esther," 335.

[9]Greenstein, "A Jewish Reading," 238–39. See also Hans Striedl, "Untersuchung zur Syntax und Stilistik des hebräischen Buches Esther," *ZAW* 55 (1937): 74, 84–85.

[10]J. Duchesne-Guillemin, "Les noms des eunuques d'Assuérus," *Muséon* 66 (1953): 105–8; rpt. in *Studies in the Book of Esther*, ed. Carey A. Moore, New York, 1982, 273–76 (hereafter this volume will be cited as Moore, *Studies*).

[11]Susan Niditch, *Underdogs and Tricksters*, San Francisco, 1987, 131.

[12]Amos Hakham, *Esther*, in *The Five Megillot* (Hebrew), *Da'at Hammiqra'*, Jerusalem, 5734/1973, 58 (hereafter this book will be identified as "Hakham").

importantly, the effect is to heighten the comic tone of the narrative. Compare the "Winken, Blinken, and Nod" of the fairy tale, or Franklin Roosevelt's "Martin, Barton, and Fish," or the ascending lists of items in the carol "The Twelve Days of Christmas," or the Passover table songs, *'eḥād mî yôdēa'* ("Who Knows One?") and *ḥad gadyā'* ("A Kid"). The two explanations are not contradictory, but complementary: One expects officialese to sound comical in a narrative that, as we shall see, seeks to lampoon the pretensions of the Persian government. Despite the seriousness of the narrative in general and the royal edicts in particular—two of them do, after all, authorize mass violence—there is always something audibly ridiculous about the imperial court. Duality again, this time the duality of high solemnity and broad humor.

3. The Messages of the Book of Esther

The book of Esther is so entertaining, so comical, and so subtle that to speak of its "message" can be profoundly misleading. Like all great literature, it demands at least that the term be in the plural: A book whose structure is amenable to many angles of vision surely has more than one message. But the more fundamental point is that unlike more straightforwardly didactic or homiletical literatures, such as Proverbs or the prophets, Esther makes most of its points by indirection. Thus its messages must be inferred. Though the action of the book is often blunt and exaggerated, its underlying attitudes, perceptions, and hopes require a more careful listening. Only in the crucial case of the observance of Purim is the point made declaratively and apodictically (9:20–32).

One attitude that pervades the book of Esther we have already mentioned— a deep skepticism about the whole Persian imperial regime. This is evident primarily in the portrayal of King Ahasuerus and the way his court functions. He is portrayed as a man of inordinate official power but no moral strength. His regime is enormously bureaucratized, yet he lacks all personal complexity. It is this disparity between the office and the man, between what he decrees and what actually happens, that imparts to the book many of its funniest scenes. But underneath the humor is a belief that the imperial administration is overblown, pompous, over-bureaucratized, and, for all its trappings of power, unable to control events. On its surface, the narrative of the book of Esther approaches the category of farce on occasion (especially in chap. 6), but the more serious category of satire always lurks behind the crude, visual humor to remind the attentive reader of the larger issues.

Chapter 1 can again serve as a pointed but not atypical example. The surviving Hebrew form of the book begins with a description of the magnitude of King Ahasuerus's realm. He rules one hundred and twenty-seven provinces from India to Nubia and commands ranks upon ranks of officers ("officials," "courtiers," "military commanders," "noblemen," and "governors" [vv. 1–3]). The author employs verbal dyads, longer strings of nouns, and other forms of redundancy to highlight the nearly inconceivable wealth at this man's command (e.g., "the vast wealth of his kingdom and the resplendent glory of his majesty" [v. 4] and especially the long lists of precious fabrics and exotic stones in v. 6). Indeed, his resources are so enormous that it takes—and he can afford—a hundred and eighty days to show it off, not to mention a second instance of comparable exhibitionism of seven days' duration (vv. 4–5). At the zenith of his success, ominously "merry with wine," Ahasuerus finds himself in the humiliating position of having his own wife refuse his invitation (vv. 10–12). He can show off the beauty of his trappings and his fabrics; that comes with the *office*. But he finds himself powerless to show off the beauty of his own wife: that comes with a *person* and requires human relations skills that he sadly and conspicuously lacks. What is still worse, he compounds the problem by treating his personal deficiency through official means, promoting an embarrassment into a state crisis and his problem with Queen Vashti into a problem of all men with their wives (vv. 13–20). The ludicrous outcome is that the man who cannot rule his wife becomes the all-powerful emperor who formally enjoins all his male subjects to rule their wives (vv. 21–22). The personal has become the political, or, to state the reverse, the political has been exposed as nothing more than the personal on solid gold stilts.

The comedy involved in Vashti's insubordination does not end with the royal decree of 1:21–22, however, but continues to ricochet in interesting ways throughout the book. For example, the man that King Ahasuerus promotes into the prime ministry reveals a strikingly similar set of weaknesses (see the commentary on chap. 3), ends up taking advice from his wife as well (5:14), and finds himself, to all appearances, powerless to refute her prediction of his doom (6:13). And the king who deposes his first wife for her insubordination ends up repeatedly deferring to her replacement, offering her up to half the empire (5:6; 7:2; cf. 9:12), and deposing and executing his prime minister because she tells him to (7:5–10). Similarly, the dialogue in which Mordecai convinces a hesitant Esther to intercede for her people concludes with *his* obeying *her* commands (chap. 4). Even in the institution of Purim, she, not he, has the last word, confirming what the two of them had previously written (9:32). The conclusion cannot be avoided: Ahasuerus and his sages' attempt to control a matter as personal and as deep-seated as gender relations by official decree proves a crashing failure.

Some of this satire is specific to the literary figure of Ahasuerus and resists generalization into a message about the Persian regime, Gentile rule, the nature of monarchy, or the like. This particular king is, after all, a weakling whose actions are always willed by his subordinates, Memucan (1:21), Haman (3:10–11), Harbona (7:9), and Esther and Mordecai (8:8). As Fox puts it, Ahasuerus "*never says no*" and "surrenders effective power to those who know how to press the right buttons—namely, his love of 'honor,' his anxiety for his authority, and his desire to appear generous."[13] But it is to be doubted that a royal figure could be portrayed in such a dismissive way were it not for a long Hebrew tradition of skepticism about monarchy and preference for a more clan- and village-centered form of social organization (e.g., Deut. 17:14–20; 1 Samuel 8; Ezek. 46:16–18). In the background of the book of Esther, one can hear overtones of the struggle in Exodus between the God of Israel and Pharaoh, who first oppresses the Israelites and slights their God (Exod. 1:8–22; 5:2) but later submits to them—and to God (e.g., 10:16–17; 12:31–32).[14] One difference between Pharaoh and Ahasuerus is, however, critical: The latter continues to rule the Jews, for the book of Esther entertains neither an expectation nor even a hope of a new exodus or of an overthrow of the Gentile powers that be. In this it is markedly different from the perspective found in Jewish apocalyptic from approximately the same period (e.g., Daniel 7), and in Christian apocalyptic as well (e.g., Revelation 17). For all its hilarious exaggeration and its gross lack of historical verisimilitude, in its perception of political life Esther exhibits a sober realism.

One surprising aspect of the political thinking of the book of Esther is its complete lack of interest in the land of Israel.[15] A comparison with the figure of Nehemiah (like Esther and Mordecai, a Jew in the Persian court at Susa) is instructive here. Hearing from his brother and some men of Judah that his people there are in dire straits and that Jerusalem's walls are in disrepair and its gates burned, Nehemiah sits, weeps, goes into mourning, prays, and fasts. When the king asks, "What is your request?" Nehemiah immediately seeks and receives a royal commission to travel to Judah to rebuild Jerusalem (Neh. 1:1–2:8). Here the contrast with Esther could not be sharper, for when the latter is asked for her request, twice with the words "[u]p to half the empire" (Esth. 5:3; 7:2; 9:12), her replies deal only with the situation at hand and never with the larger historical plight of the Jews. The situation at hand is, of course, a mortal crisis and therefore more pressing than the long-standing questions of the exile and the status of the Jews in the Holy Land, but the total focus on the empire and the absence of concern with Jerusalem and its Temple are most unusual. They seem to be a piece with the relatively high estimation of Gentile rule in Esther, or, to put it differently, with the definition of Jewish success as consisting of the presence of Jews in high places able to influence a non-Jew-

---

[13]Fox, *Character,* 173.

[14]See Gilles Gerleman, *Esther,* BKAT, Neukirchen-Vluyn, 1973, 11–23 (hereafter this book will be identified as "Gerleman").

[15]See Jon D. Levenson, "The Scroll of Esther in Ecumenical Perspective," *JES* 13 (1976): 440–51.

The King's Library

ish emperor. There are, in short, two remarkable characteristics to the sociopolitical dimension of the book of Esther: first, that it includes no vision of the overthrow of foreign power and, second, that even the dramatic and perhaps miraculous transformation that does take place involves only the squelching of anti-Semitism, not the restoration of the land of Israel or the reversal of the exile.

The reason for this particular anomaly is unclear. Part of the answer may involve the rather naturalistic theology of the book (on which see pp. 17–21 below), which has some affinities with the worldview of wisdom literature.[16] Consider, for example, the book of Qohelet (Ecclesiastes) in its similar disinterest in cosmic transformation or in the particularities of Jewish religious existence and its focus, instead, on the repeating cycles that define the inescapable and unending rhythm of all human life. Qohelet and the surviving Hebrew form of Esther (whose authors may well have been contemporaries) are alike in their absence of dramatic divine intervention into the course of human events and their almost total disinterest, so far as we can tell, in the liturgical life of the Jewish people (see, e.g., Qoh. 9:2). But the analogy ends there, and if wisdom literature has influenced Esther—after all, Haman and Mordecai are almost the stereotypical foolish and wise courtiers, respectively—it is not the skeptical wisdom of Qohelet, but a vastly more optimistic and imaginative variety and one that is not at all skittish about Jewish particularism. In summary, even if some of Esther's lack of interest in the land of Israel can be ascribed to its affinities to cosmopolitan wisdom literature, the explanation is not exhaustive, and the anomaly of its conclusion continues to press upon us.

Another explanation may derive from the provenance of the book. It is quite possible that in Esther we have a rare glimpse into the thinking of Jews in the eastern Diaspora in the mid-Second Temple period (on the dating, see section 4, below). Surely not all of these thought like Nehemiah; few would have attempted to visit Jerusalem, let alone rebuild it. Whereas what interests the authors of Ezra and Nehemiah is the careers of those two men in the land of Israel and the earlier Persian actions that made their careers possible, what interests the author of Esther is Jewish life in the Diaspora and the Persian actions that make it sustainable and successful. Though we cannot be certain of either its date or its place of composition, it would seem reasonable to assume that the book of Esther is a legacy of Persian Jewry and reflects a stratum of society with a very different understanding of Jewishness from that of comparable literature. This is a stratum that has come to terms with diaspora, and, indeed, the book of Esther can be read as the story of the transformation of the *exile* into the *Diaspora*. If its author hopes for something beyond the

---

[16]See Shemaryahu Talmon, " 'Wisdom' in the Book of Esther," *VT* (1963): 419–55; rpt. in *Studies in the Hebrew Bible,* Jerusalem and Leiden, 1993, 255–90.

normalization and empowerment of diaspora Jewry, if he hopes for a messianic advent or an apocalyptic overthrow of Gentile power and a triumphant restoration of the elect to their promised land and to divine service in the Temple, he gives no hint of it.

In this light, the figure of Mordecai reflects not only the political wisdom of a successful courtier loyal to his people, and the figure of Esther not only the charm and eloquence of a successful consort who courageously intervenes in defense of her people: Both figures also personify the transformation of the Jews that the narrative in its larger outline reflects—or, perhaps more accurately, *fantasizes,* since we have no evidence that the transformation depicted occurred outside the fictive world of the book of Esther itself. Mordecai is an exile from Judah who, by adhering to his ancestral traditions in defiance of the king's command and at the risk of life itself, saves the lives of his people and becomes both second to the king and the beloved advocate of the Jews (2:5–6; 3:1–6; 10:3). Esther is not only an exile, but an orphan and a person who must disguise her ethnicity. Yet through good luck of mysterious origin, great personal courage, obedience to her foster father, and rare eloquence, she too rises to royal estate and effects the deliverance of her threatened nation. Those transformations from refugee to prime minister and from orphan to queen recall prophetic visions of restoration after exile (e.g., Isaiah 54) and suggest that Mordecai and Esther, for all their particular character, are also allegorizations of Israel's national destiny. Given their eminence, they cannot be representative Jews, but they are representative of the Jewish people collectively, at least according to the hopes and fantasies of the author of the book. The course of their lives recalls two other Israelite/Jewish exiles who rise in foreign courts, Joseph and Daniel. But in their personification of the national hopes, they recall Judith even more, whose name means "the Jewess" and whose transformation from a widow fasting for her beleaguered people (Judith 9) into their savior singing a hymn of triumph (chap. 16) reflects the astonishing change in the fate of the nation whose name she bears.

Though the book of Esther has abundant affinities with the stories of Joseph, Daniel, and Judith, it is the first of these three figures whose social situation most resembles that of Mordecai and Esther. As Berg points out, "[t]he Joseph story . . . reflects an accommodation to life in a diaspora setting [and] points to the possibility for a rewarding and fruitful life outside Palestine [as well as] the possibility of an Israelite's concern for both his own people and his foreign master."[17] As always in Jewish history, the accommodation is dangerous and fragile and requires that the Jews be alert to the resentment that their differentness and their dual loyalties provoke. Part of the message of the book of Esther is that Jewish survival requires not only active identification of Jewish in-

---

[17]Berg, *The Book,* 175.

dividuals with the well-being of their people, but also constant vigilance, political wisdom, and extraordinary courage. That the book anticipated a Gentile readership is unlikely, but it does carry a message for Gentiles as well: The Jews will survive even when the odds against them are staggering; those who are kind to the Jews will prosper as a result; and the enemies of the Jews will eventually be destroyed (cf. Gen. 12:3). It is not a message that the nations of the world, even those who regard Esther as sacred scripture, have generally been inclined to heed.

What guarantees this message is unclear. The presence of Esther in the Bible leads us (usually more subtly than we recognize) to identify the power that brings about its happy conclusion with the God of Israel. Read in this fashion, Esther is a variety of the familiar tale of God's chosen cast into desperate straits and then rescued by their divine savior. This is how Jewish tradition has historically understood the book, beginning already with its Septuagintal recension (see below, section 5). One oft-remarked point suggests, however, that the canonical status of Esther can be misleading: unlike those other stories of affliction and deliverance, including the obviously comparable tales of Joseph, Moses, Daniel, and Judith, no name of God appears in the surviving Hebrew form of the book of Esther. Though various explanations to mitigate this anomaly have been proposed,[18] they are all apologetic and unconvincing. As a result, many scholars have pronounced the book to be irredeemably secular. Cornill, for example, terms it "an entirely profane history" and Bernhard Anderson finds in it a "nationalism . . . in complete indifference to God."[19]

What makes a piece of literature secular or religious is a more complex issue than Esther's modern detractors have usually realized. Fox points out that the identification of nationalism with secularity is anachronistic: "It is unlikely that such an attitude would have been comprehensible in the ancient world."[20] Indeed, as the author of this commentary has elsewhere pointed out, the particularism of the book of Esther is no greater than that of most of the books of the Hebrew Bible (e.g., Exodus) and the New Testament (e.g., Romans), and "if universalism is our theological goal, our problems do not begin with Esther."[21]

More to the point is the absence of religious rites in the book. For example, though we hear of crying, sackcloth and ashes, and fasting (Esth. 4:1–3, 16), we find in the Hebrew version neither prayers nor even a statement that these

---

[18]See Fox, *Character,* 238–40.

[19]C. H. Cornill, *Einleitung in das Alte Testament,* Leipzig, 1891, 153; Bernhard W. Anderson, "The Place of the Book of Esther in the Christian Bible," *JR* 30 (1950): 40. On this, see Levenson, "The Scroll," 440–44, and Fox, *Character,* 235–36.

[20]Fox, *Character,* 236.

[21]Levenson, "The Scroll," 442. See also Jon D. Levenson, "The Universal Horizon of Biblical Particularism," in *Ethnicity and the Bible,* ed. Mark G. Brett, Leiden, 1996, 143–69.

rites of affliction are undertaken in order to induce the Deity to cancel the evil decree (see the commentary on 4:12–17). This is a gap that the Jewish tradition has richly and variously filled, beginning again with the redaction that appears in the Septuagint (see especially chap. C). Yet this very move testifies to the anomaly of a biblical book that avails itself of none of the many names of God in the tradition, even when it reports what appear to be religious rituals. Note also that if the three-day fast of 4:16 follows immediately upon the issuance of the genocidal edict on the thirteenth day of the first month (3:12), then we have the further oddity of the Jews' fasting on Passover, which begins in the evening of the fourteenth (Lev. 23:5). Indeed, given the chronology of the narrative, the absence of all mention of Passover is another anomaly. It would seem to be akin to the lack of attention to Jewish dietary law, a matter of explicit concern, by contrast, in Daniel and Judith (Dan. 1:6–16; Judith 12:2). Even more amazing is Esther's marriage to a Gentile (cf. Ezra 9:1–2; Neh. 10:31; 13:23–28). This is still odder if one understands Esth. 8:17 to show that Gentiles might convert to Judaism, as Ahasuerus does not (see the commentary on Esth. 8:17).

All of this suggests considerable distance from the sacral institutions of ancient Israel, especially as these were developing in the Second Temple period, during which Esther was composed. If we transfer our attention, however, from novellas to wisdom literature (with which, as we have seen, the book of Esther has some affinities), its anomalousness appears diminished. If Qohelet, for example, had written a narrative instead of a collection of sayings, the result would probably have been as remote from the liturgical life and perhaps even the traditional law of the Jews as Esther is. This should not be pushed too far, however, for the book of Esther does serve as the etiological legend for a festival (9:20–32) and should not therefore be seen as altogether divorced from the liturgical life. And should it be retorted that the earliest version of the book made no reference to Purim, it can be rejoined that the same version also made explicit reference to God (see below, section 5). If secularity be defined as the absence of mention of the Deity or of religious institutions, then we must say that at no point in its compositional history was the book of Esther secular.

But is God really of no concern in the book of Esther? That he is unnamed need not entail that he is uninvolved. Indeed, one might suspect that he is responsible for the extraordinary pattern of apparent coincidences that characterizes the narrative and makes possible the deliverance of the Jews from seemingly certain extermination.[22] Fox lists these as follows: "the timely vacancy of the queenship at the Persian court, the opportune accession of a Jew to queenship, Mordecai's discovery of the eunuchs' conspiracy, Esther's favor-

---

[22]On this, see D.J.A. Clines, *The Esther Scroll*, JSOTSup 30, Sheffield, 1984, 153–58 (hereafter this book will be abbreviated as "Clines").

able reception by the king, the king's insomnia, Haman's early arrival at the palace, and Haman's reckless plea for mercy at Esther's feet." We must reckon, moreover, not only with the individual coincidences but with the elaborate and highly improbably symmetrical pattern in which they have been embedded (see the figure on p. 8). Fox is correct that "[n]umerous stories shamelessly heap up improbable coincidences without investing them with theological significance—*As You Like It, The Marriage of Figaro,* and *Bleak House,* for example,"[23] but they must not be so numerous in Second Temple Judaism or Fox would surely have cited at least one example from that large body of literature as well. It is more reasonable to assume that the author endorsed the old saw that "a coincidence is a miracle in which God prefers to remain anonymous."

In fact, the idea that the seeming coincidences of the narrative have been arranged by some higher power—higher than the individual event itself and higher than the fates that Haman consulted by casting the lot (*pûr*)—is explicit in the text itself. First, consider Mordecai's reply when Esther hesitates to approach the king:

> Don't imagine that you alone of all the Jews will escape because you are in the king's palace. On the contrary, if you really do remain silent in such a time as this, relief and deliverance will arise for the Jews from another quarter, but you and your father's family will perish. And who knows? Perhaps it is just for such an occasion as this that you have attained to royal estate! (4:13–14)

On the basis of a hardheaded—or should we say "secular"?—analysis of the crisis at hand, Mordecai's conviction that "relief and deliverance will arise for the Jews" seems uncharacteristically simpleminded. And how does he know that Esther and her father's family—probably including himself—will perish when that happens? One need not see the term "quarter" (*māqôm*) as a name of God (which it will become in the rabbinic period) to suspect that the source of deliverance and retribution to which Mordecai alludes is indeed the Deity, and not "Jewry's inner strength and potential for self-help," as Fox would have it.[24] For it was not inner strength or self-help that accounted for Esther's ascendancy to royal estate, but rather the opportune dethronement of Vashti, Esther's innate beauty, and, especially, the favor the latter unaccountably evoked in Hegai, the harem-keeper (2:8–9, 15). And if Mordecai really is alluding only to "Jewry's inner strength and potential for self-help," Esther must be misinterpreting him, for she first signals her acceptance of the assignment by calling for a citywide fast among the Jews of Susa (4:16)—a totally impotent and senseless gesture if there is no higher power that it can influence.

---

[23]Fox, *Character,* 241.
[24]Ibid., 244.

Slightly less explicit than 4:13–14, the second allusion to a higher power that has arranged events to the benefit of the Jews occurs in 6:13, a crucial verse that we have had repeated occasion to cite: "[Haman's] advisers and his wife Zeresh said to him, 'If Mordecai, before whom you have begun to fall, is of Jewish descent, you will never overcome him. You shall collapse altogether before him.' (Esth. 6:13b)." The translation of *'im* as "if" here can be misleading, for Haman's advisers and his wife already know that Mordecai is indeed Jewish (5:13). All that has changed since they advised the prime minister to impale his nemesis is the public acclamation of Mordecai and humiliation of Haman in chap. 6. Given the magnitude of his ego-needs, that event is deeply traumatic to Haman, but it need not imply the triumph of the Jews in general or his own downfall. After all, his advisers and Zeresh are almost certainly ignorant of Esther's Jewishness and thus have no more reason than he to suspect that his second banquet with the king and queen will eventuate in his death sentence. The tone of 6:13b is as confident and as definitive as Mordecai's prediction of deliverance and retribution in 4:14 and just as inappropriate to the situation at hand—unless, of course, the situation at hand is part of a larger pattern that can work only to the benefit of the Jews. The prediction that Haman's advisers and his wife make in 6:13b is thus best seen as an interpretation of the preceding parade as an *omen,* an event that discloses a larger and inevitable pattern. Fox puts it well: "There is a logic in history beyond natural causality, and this allows the wise (as Haman's friends are called) to discern the direction history is moving in."[25]

It is not only the wise, however, who discern the "logic in history beyond natural causality." By the end of the tale, Gentiles are "identif[ying] themselves with the Jews because the fear of the Jews had fallen upon them" (8:17). Even the anti-Semites are powerless, "for the fear of them [i.e., the Jews again] had fallen upon all people," and all manner of royal officials "gave honor to the Jews because the fear of Mordecai fell upon them" (9:2–3). The grace that makes its first appearance in the story when Esther wins the favor of Hegai the harem-keeper (2:9; cf. v. 15) has now been extended to Mordecai and, finally, to *all* the Jews as well.[26] In these cases, the "logic in history beyond natural causality" manifests itself not only in the larger pattern in which the individual event is embedded, but also in the event itself. For surely this degree of fear of the minority by the majority is so inexplicable by natural causality that the term "miracle"—with all due qualification—applies.

To Fox, "awareness of this logic [in history beyond natural causality] does

---

[25]Ibid., 246.

[26]See Arndt Meinhold, "Theologische Erwägungen zum Buch Esther," *TZ* 34 (1978): 321–33, esp. 325–26.

not require or lead to a particular theology."[27] This depends, of course, on what one defines as theology. If the definition requires explicit mention of God, then Fox wins the point. If, on the other hand, theology deals with the character of ultimate reality and its manifestation in human history, then Mordecai, Haman's advisers, and Zeresh have articulated the theology of the book of Esther fairly completely: A hidden force arranges events in such a way that even against the most daunting odds the Jews are protected and delivered. The hiddenness of the force is an essential part of this theology, for, as Berg puts it, "the narrator believed in a hidden causality behind the surface of human history, both concealing and governing the order and significance of events."[28] If, influenced by the scriptural status that Esther has attained, we call that "hidden causality" God, we must be all the more careful to differentiate God as he appears in this narrative from the God of so much of biblical tradition, whose presence is visible, audible, and dramatic. Esther's God is one who works behind the scenes, carefully arranging events so that a justice based on the principle of "measure for measure" will triumph and the Jews will survive and flourish. There is an intriguing parallel between this description of God and the figure of Mordecai, who speaks only two verses (4:13–14) but carefully (though at first inexplicably) sets things up so that Haman will be disgraced, the Jews rescued, and Mordecai himself elevated. There is also an obvious parallel once more to the Joseph story of Genesis 37–50, in which God never appears or speaks to the hero and yet envelops him in a grace that repeatedly wins him favor and eventually enables him to decode the unlikely events of his life as a providential plan to keep the Israelite nation alive despite famine (Gen. 39:2–5; 45:5; 50:20).[29] In Fox's eloquent words, "[t]he willingness to face history with an openness to the possibility of providence—even when history seems to weigh against its likelihood, as it did in the dark days after the issuance of Haman's decree—this is a stance of profound faith."[30] It is, I submit, a profounder and more realistic stance of faith than that of most of biblical tradition.

Bearing in mind our caution that except on the issue of Purim, the book of Esther is not overtly didactic and any lessons it teaches must be inferred, we can state its main messages this way: In a world in which arrogant and fickle

---

[27]Fox, *Character,* 246. But note Fox's ambivalence: "I myself have gone back and forth" (244).

[28]Berg, *The Book,* 178.

[29]See Jon D. Levenson, *The Death and Resurrection of the Beloved Son,* New Haven, Conn., 1993, 143–69. The only direct address of God in Genesis 37–50 is to Jacob in Beer-sheba on his way to Egypt (46:2–4). Joseph's decoding of his experience as an enactment of the logic of providence may be owing to the special grace that attends him, but it is surely not owing to any verbal or visual revelation.

[30]Fox, *Character,* 242.

regimes seek a control of events that they have not been granted, and in which the differentness of the Jews provokes murderous hostility, the Jews can, through their own wisdom and courage and with lucky happenstances ordained by a sovereign and favoring providence, defeat their would-be murderers, secure their position, rise to eminence, and even benefit Gentile kings in the process.

All these inferred messages are, however, secondary to the explicit point of the book of Esther in the forms in which it has been handed down in Judaism and Christianity: that Jews shall "keep these two days in the prescribed manner and at their appointed time every year . . . and that these days of Purim [shall] never leave the midst of the Jews nor the memory of them cease among their descendants" (9:27–28). Though scholars have long speculated about a wide variety of possible non-Jewish origins for Purim,[31] the book itself (perhaps tendentiously) maintains that the origin of the festival lies in the events therein narrated, and the speculations are for that reason more relevant to the history of the Jewish religion than to the exegesis of Esther. Three of the four most important aspects of the observance of Purim that are developed in the rabbinic tradition are mentioned in the book of Esther itself: "banqueting . . . sending presents of food to each other and gifts to the poor" (v. 22). The banquet must be held in the daytime (in the afternoon unless Purim falls on Friday, in which case the banquet is advanced to the morning out of deference to the Sabbath). Needless to say, in keeping with the spirit of the occasion, the meal is joyous and normally there is liberal consumption of alcohol. The rabbinic requirement as to the "presents of food [that Jews are to send] to each other" involves a minimum of two types of food, ready to be eaten and sent to one person. The "gifts to the poor" involve a minimum of one gift to each of two impoverished individuals. All of these commandments can and usually do surpass these minimums. They are incumbent on Jewish men and women alike.[32]

The same is true for the one commandment of Purim as the Talmudic rabbis developed it that is not found in the book of Esther—the obligation of publicly reading the book itself.[33] This is done twice, on the evening and on the morning of Purim (the Jewish day begins in the evening). The reading must be done from a specially prepared scroll, known as a *megillah* (Hebrew, *měgillâ*, "scroll"). Although other biblical books are sometimes called *megillot* (plural

---

[31]See, e.g., Lewis Bayles Paton, *A Critical and Exegetical Commentary on the Book of Esther*, ICC, Edinburgh, 1908, 77–94 (hereafter this book will be identified as "Paton"); Theodore H. Gaster, *Purim and Hanukkah in Custom and Tradition*, New York, 1950, 6–18; Carey A. Moore, *Esther*, AB 7B, Garden City, N.Y., 1971, xlvi–xlix (hereafter this book will be identified as "Moore, *Esther*"), and Gerleman, 23–28.

[32]See the *Mishnah Berurah*, par. 694–95.

[33]See the *Mishnah Berurah*, par. 689–90.

of *megillah*), the term *megillah* alone has come to mean the book of Esther in its Hebrew form. As one would expect, the observance of Purim keeps Esther in mind, and the public chanting of Esther ensures, in turn, that Purim maintains its traditional character.

4. Historicity
and Date of Composition

The narrative of the book of Esther takes place in the time of the ancient Persian empire, which rose to eminence with its defeat of Babylonia in 539 B.C.E. and fell to Alexander the Great of Macedon in 333 B.C.E. The Persian king is called "Ahasuerus," which seems to be how Hebrew speakers heard the Persian name that the Greeks rendered as Xerxes. Xerxes, who is well-known from several Greek sources (but especially Herodotus), reigned from 486–465 B.C.E.. The Jewish hero Mordecai is identified as a man "who had been exiled from Jerusalem with the group that was carried into exile along with Jeconiah, king of Judah, whom Nebuchadnezzar, king of Babylon, had driven into exile" (2:6), referring to the catastrophe of 597 B.C.E. (2 Kings 24:8–17), ten years before the greater catastrophe of the destruction of Jerusalem and the loss of the Davidic monarchy (2 Kings 25:1–26).

Even without the synchronisms that derive from extrabiblical sources, one can detect grave chronological problems in the book of Esther. A man who was born at least ten years before the Babylonians razed Jerusalem figures as a principal protagonist in a story that takes place a generation or two after the Babylonians have, in turn, been overthrown by the Persians. If one brings those extrabiblical synchronisms to bear, Mordecai is a minimum of 114 years old when the action of the book of Esther begins in Xerxes's third year (1:3). If one is determined, as some religious traditionalists are, to read the book as an accurate historical report, one is forced to understand 2:6 as referring not to the exile of Mordecai himself, but of his great-grandfather, Kish (v. 5).

Even if we make this questionable adjustment, the historical problems with Esther are so massive as to persuade anyone who is not already obligated by religious dogma to believe in the historicity of biblical narrative to doubt the veracity of the narrative.[34] First, it must be noted that no evidence whatsoever for any of the key events of the book of Esther has ever turned up. The *megillah* correlates with no other biblical or extrabiblical information. Now it is surely true that "absence of evidence is not evidence of absence," and it may be that tomorrow's archaeological discovery will make obsolete the previous sentence. This is possible, but highly unlikely, for we have a large amount of

---

[34]Discussions of the historical problem of Esther are many. See, e.g., Paton, 64–77; Moore, *Esther,* xxxiv–xlvi; and Fox, *Character,* 131–39.

evidence about the Persian period and Xerxes in particular, and the best face for the historicity of Esther that one can put on this evidence is that the author of the book sometimes shows some familiarity with details of life in the Persian empire. The author knows, for example, about its size, its postal system, and a considerable number of details about its court life (3:13; 8:10) and employs a number of words and a few names of indisputable Persian origin.[35] These last include "Mordecai," which is almost certainly identical to "Mardukâ." This name, "in an undated text coming probably from either the last years of Darius or the first years of Xerxes," appears as "an accountant who was a member of an inspection tour from Susa."[36] Given its association with the Babylonian god-name "Marduk," one should not be surprised to find the name of Mordecai paralleled in literature of this period, but the notion that Mardukâ in the Persian inscription and the Mordecai of the book of Esther are the same individual strains credulity and cannot be used to support the historicity of the biblical book (though it often has been). One might as well argue that the appearance of the name "George" as a colonist in North America in the eighteenth century proves accurate the old story of Washington and the cherry tree. To Ungnad's claim, "[t]hat there were two officials with the same name at the same time in the same place is scarcely likely," Fox's retort is compelling: "[w]ere this supposition valid, it could just as well prove that the Mordecai of our book did *not* exist."[37]

Esther herself is even more of a historical improbability. According to Herodotus (3:84), the Persian king could marry only within seven noble families, and there is, needless to say, no reason to think that any of them were Jewish. In addition, we know that Xerxes's wife was named "Amēstris" (7:114; 9:112). The name may vaguely suggest that of Esther (perhaps also to the author of the *megillah*), but the chronology again refutes the identification with either of Ahasuerus's queens. As Fox points out, "Amēstris accompanied Xerxes to Sardis in 480 and was still acting very much as queen."[38] This is after Vashti had been deposed in Xerxes's third year (Esth. 1:3) but before Esther was enthroned as her successor in his seventh (2:16–18). In summary, there is even less evidence for Esther (and Vashti) as historical figures than for Mordecai.

Alongside the realia of the Persian court that the book of Esther reports accurately, there are a number that contradict our knowledge from classical sources or from common sense. There is, for example, no evidence for the existence of 127 provinces or satrapies (1:1; 8:9). Various Persian inscriptions

[35]See Moore, *Esther,* xli, and idem, "Esther, Book of," *ABD* 2:638.

[36]Moore, *Esther,* l. See Arthur Ungnad, "Keilinschriftliche Beiträge zum Buch Ezra und Esther," *ZAW* 58 (1940–41): 244.

[37]Arthur Ungnad, *ZAW* 59 (1942–43): 219; Fox, *Character,* 135.

[38]Fox, *Character,* 136.

mention twenty-three, twenty-four, twenty-nine, and thirty, for Xerxes's father Darius. The book of Daniel tells of 120 (Dan. 6:2). Herodotus gives us the figure of twenty satrapies for Xerxes's own empire (3:89).[39] Or, to give another example, the notion, prominent in Esther (1:19; 8:8) and likewise in Daniel (6:9, 13, 16), that a law of the Persians and Medes is irrevocable, is without external corroboration and would seem utterly impractical. In both Esther and Daniel, one can reasonably suspect that the biblical sources are embellishing or creating facts in the service of their exquisite narratives rather than conveying accurate data in the service of dry empirical history. This is also the case for such unlikely data as the banquet that lasts 180 days (Esth. 1:1–4), the decrees that go out in a multitude of languages rather than in Aramaic, the lingua franca of the Persian empire (1:22; 3:12; 8:9), the edict authorizing the annihilation of an entire people almost a year hence (3:8–15), and the report of the Jews' slaughtering 75,510 anti-Semites without indication of any losses of their own (9:11–16).

What all this argues is that the book of Esther is best seen as a historical novella set within the Persian empire. This is not to say that the book is false, only that its truth, like the truth of any piece of literature, is relative to its genre, and the genre of Esther is not that of the historical annal (though it sometimes imitates the style of a historical annal).[40] For this reason, it is misleading to translate Ahasuerus's name as "Xerxes," since that implies some correlation with the figure known from the Greek sources. Instead, it would seem that the author borrowed Xerxes's name but little else about him in order to create the novella. This reuse of old names in ways that do not square with the historical data is altogether characteristic of Second Temple Jewish literature, and probably of older Israelite literature as well. Fox offers as an analogy the book of Judith, in which Nebuchadnezzar rules Assyria from Nineveh (Judith 1:1), though he was actually king of Babylonia and assumed the throne about seven years after Nineveh had been destroyed.[41] In the case of Esther, however, there is more of an effort to convey an ambience authentic to the period in which the events are said to have taken place, and the Persian customs, words, and names suggest greater familiarity with the period of the narrative than we find in most Second Temple literature, including Daniel and Judith.

When the book of Esther was written is unknown. Fox finds it "unlikely that a writer would refer to the 127 satrapies of Persia while the Persian empire was still in existence, any more than a modern work about the United States would be accepted as history if it spoke of the 300 States of the Union."[42] This may well be true, but we have no idea how widely known the number of satrapies

[39]Ibid., 132 n. 4.
[40]On the genre of Esther, see ibid., 141–52.
[41]Ibid., 134.
[42]Ibid., 139.

was in the Persian empire, among either Persians or Jews, nor can we be sure that the readership of the book cared. An analogy from the book of Judith may be useful here. That composition is highly dependent on older biblical narratives, yet it uses the name of Nebuchadnezzar in ways that any Bible readers would instantly spot as inaccurate—if, that is, they really cared to think so empirically. Though Esther has usually been taken as historical reportage, we cannot be sure that was its author's intention. I am not persuaded by Fox's claim that "the author . . . almost certainly meant us to read the book as a precise report of actual historical events."[43] How exactly an ancient religious community—or a modern one—understands "actual historical events" is a complicated epistemological and hermeneutical issue. The enormous amount of exaggeration and inaccuracy in Esther suggests a motive other than precise reporting in the modern, Western sense.[44]

Since Ahasuerus has to be identified with a gloss (Esth. 1:1), he does seem to be a figure from the past. In addition, there is some linguistic evidence for placing Esther later in the Second Temple period rather than earlier.[45] Against this, however, one must note its positive attitude toward a Gentile king: when the happy ending arrives, Ahasuerus is still on his throne, Esther is apparently still his queen, and Mordecai is his prime minister (chap. 10). This contrasts strikingly with much Jewish literature stemming from after the Seleucid persecution and the Hasmonean rebellion (167–165 B.C.E.) and the establishment of a Jewish dynasty in Judah soon thereafter. All of this suggests a date of composition at some distance from the time of Xerxes but before the watershed of the mid-second century B.C.E..

The book of Esther was thus probably written in the fourth or third century B.C.E., but the dearth of Jewish literature that can be securely dated to those centuries and the complete absence of compositions known to come from Persian Jewry in antiquity make it extremely difficult to place the book within the frameworks and typologies that are available. The author's focus on Susa suggests that city as the locus of composition. See especially 9:19, which, as Fox notes, "assumes the Susan date of Purim (15 Adar) and explains the non-Susan one (14 Adar)."[46] If the book of Esther is of Persian origin, it may well be the sole surviving legacy of a Jewish culture very different from those of either Palestine or the rest of the Diaspora.

When the book became known in the West is also unclear. In the list of the

[43]Ibid., 138.

[44]See Greenstein, "A Jewish," 226–28, for an argument that the interpretation of Esther as history misunderstands its comic, festive nature.

[45]See Ron Bergey, "Late Linguistic Features in Esther," *JQR* 85 (1984): 66–78, esp. 72, 75–76.

[46]Fox, *Character,* 140. This assumes the inauthenticity of the LXX plus to 9:19. See our philological note to that verse.

great heroes of Israel in the Wisdom of Joshua ben Sira (Ecclesiasticus), written in the early second century B.C.E., Mordecai and Esther are conspicuous for their absence (Sir. 44–50), but in 2 Maccabees, which probably dates from late in the same century, we find 14 Adar called "the Day of Mordecai" (2 Macc. 15:36), which suggests that the story and the observance of Purim had by then become familiar in the West.[47] In any event, the colophon to the Septuagint version of Esther tells of the arrival in Egypt of some Greek form of the book in the fourth year of the reign of Ptolemy and Cleopatra, though which couple by that name is not specified (F:11). As indicated in the commentary, the possible dates range from 114–13 to 78–77 B.C.E.. It can safely be assumed that Esther and Purim were known to Palestinian Jewry by early in the first century B.C.E..

5. Versions

Of the different versions of the book of Esther that may have existed in antiquity, only two are still in general circulation, and they correspond to two divergent biblical canons. The first version we may call the "Masoretic," after the Hebrew word for "tradition." The Masoretic Text (MT) is the form of the Hebrew Bible handed down through rabbinic tradition and thereby endowed with canonical status among Jews. It is this form of Esther to which I have been referring as "the surviving Hebrew form," to distinguish it from the Greek version, known as the Septuagint and indicated by the Roman numeral for seventy (LXX). In the main, the Greek version is itself a translation of a lost Hebrew original that was quite close to the MT but not, as we shall see, identical to it. Within the LXX, however, there are six passages for which no Hebrew original survives, and these six passages define the essential difference between the Jews and Protestants, on the one hand, and the Eastern Orthodox and Roman Catholics, on the other, on the text of Esther.

Finding no Hebrew versions of these six Septuagintal passages, the church father Jerome (fourth century C.E.) doubted their authenticity and relegated them to the end of the book of Esther in the Vulgate, his new Latin translation of the Christian Bible. In that location they lost much of their meaning, since they are there deprived of their natural and original placement in the narrative. The Protestant Reformers of the sixteenth century C.E. decanonized these Latin texts for which no Hebrew original existed (and over which doubt had long hovered), and the Protestant traditions have generally labeled them as "Apocrypha," that is, "hidden books." Hence, one finds a book of the Apocrypha called the "Additions to Esther," though no such freestanding document had

---

[47]See Shemaryahu Talmon, "Was the Book of Esther Known at Qumran?" *DSD* 2 (1995): 249–67.

ever existed. In response, the Council of Trent (1546) reiterated the canonical status of the six "Additions," and they remain an authentic part of the Roman Catholic Old Testament to this day. Among Eastern Christians, though the canonicity of Esther in any form was long disputed,[48] it is the LXX version, with the "Additions" in their original places, that is authoritative.

Like the books of Daniel and Jeremiah, which have a similar history, Esther poses a nettlesome problem to translators and commentators who write for an interfaith readership. Were we to take only the MT as our subject, we would privilege the Jewish and Protestant traditions at the expense of the Roman Catholic and Eastern Orthodox. Were we to adopt the LXX as our text, we would present a version of the book of Esther familiar only to the last of these four groups. Were we to place the six Greek passages without surviving Hebrew originals at the end of our volume or to relegate them to a different book in our commentary series altogether (as most series do), we would present them in a decontextualized form that does justice neither to them nor to the Christian traditions that continue to revere the LXX. The compromise represented by this Old Testament Library commentary is as follows. Wherever the MT exists, it is translated and commented upon. The Greek pluses are treated the same way and left in their original locations. The only difference is that they are given chapter letters (A–F) rather than numbers, are printed in italics, and are set apart in our table of contents of the book of Esther (see pp. v–vii). My hope in this is to do substantial justice to all versions of Esther currently in general circulation and to minimize as far as possible the inevitable privileging of some traditions over others.

Since sections 1–4 of our introduction have dealt only with the MT, it is necessary here to add comments about the "Additions." Chap. A, which precedes chap. 1 of the MT, begins with Mordecai's ominous dream of fearsome combat by or between two dragons (vv. 1–7). At this, "the entire race of the just were dismayed," expecting to be annihilated, but then "a great river . . . issued . . . from a small spring," the sun came out, and they were rescued (vv. 8–10). The next night Mordecai overheard two eunuchs, Gabatha and Tharra, plotting to assassinate King Artaxerxes (as he is called throughout the LXX). Mordecai informs on them and is rewarded with a position at court. Because of this, Haman seeks to do Mordecai in (vv. 11–18).

Chapter B, which comes between 3:13 and 3:14, is the text of the edict of genocide against the Jews. In it, King Artaxerxes rehearses his wish to rule equitably and humanely (vv. 1–3). As an example of how he will bring this about, he points to a warning from Haman (whom he praises to the sky) about a certain unspecified nationality that is misanthropic and disobedient to the king (v. 4). Artaxerxes orders that nation, including their wives and children, annihi-

---

[48]See Moore, *Esther,* xxv–xxviii.

lated on the *fourteenth* of Adar (vv. 5–7), a date one finds several times in various non-Masoretic manuscripts (whereas the MT consistently reads the thirteenth).[49]

Chapter C, which falls between 4:17 and chap. D, records the prayers of the two heroes of the tale. Mordecai's prayer (vv. 1–10) affirms God's omnipotence, defends Mordecai against the charge of arrogance in refusing to bow to Haman, and calls upon the God of Abraham to rescue the latter's descendants from obliteration. Esther's prayer (vv. 14–30) sounds similar notes, though in more detail. In it, the queen also asks for the courage and the eloquence to sway the king and defends herself against the charge that she enjoys having sex with non-Jews or eating their food.

Chapter D follows C and precedes 5:1, though it overlaps in content with 5:1–3. Chapter D records Esther's fearful approach to the king at the risk of her very life (vv. 1–6). Staggering, she nearly passes out, but God changes the king's spirit to gentleness, and Artaxerxes tenderly revives and reassures her (vv. 7–11). Nonetheless, she faints again, to the alarm of all (vv. 13–15).

Chapter E, which intervenes between 8:12 and 8:13, is the text of Artaxerxes's pro-Jewish edict. In it, the king accuses Haman of ingratitude and speaks of the "evil-hating judgment of the God who always sees everything" (vv. 2–4). In fact, Haman is not even a Persian, but a Macedonian plotting to do in the king's loyal benefactor, Mordecai, and the royal consort, Esther, in order to betray Persia to Macedonia (vv. 10–14). The Jews are exonerated of the charge of disobedience and identified as God's chosen people (vv. 15–16). Finally, the *thirteenth* of Adar is elevated to the status of a festival (vv. 19–23), unlike the MT, where Purim is celebrated on the fourteenth or fifteenth.

Finally, chapter F, which ends the LXX of Esther, presents Mordecai's decoding of his initial premonitory dream in terms of the events recorded in the book of Esther itself. The deliverance of the Jews is attributed to God (vv. 1–6), and *Purim,* the plural of the word for "lot," is interpreted as referring to two lots, "one for the people of God and one for all the nations" (vv. 7–8). Chapter F closes with a colophon telling of the arrival from Jerusalem to Egypt of some form of the Greek book of Esther (v. 11).

There is no reason to assume that the six "Additions to Esther" stem from the same hand. Indeed, whereas A, C, and D are probably translations of a Hebrew or Aramaic original, B and E are almost certainly original compositions, which F may or may not be.[50] Nonetheless, implanted within the MT or a close

---

[49]See Michael V. Fox, *The Redaction of the Books of Esther,* SBLMS 40, Atlanta, 1991, 80–81 n. 84.

[50]R. A. Martin, "Syntax Criticism of the LXX Additions to Esther," *JBL* 94 (1975) 65–72; rpt. in *Studies in the Book of Esther,* ed. Carey A. Moore, New York, 1982, 595–602.

Greek relative of it, these texts reinforce the bilateral chiastic structure of the MT (see figure 2, p. 8 above), as can be best rendered with another V-shaped diagram (figure 3).

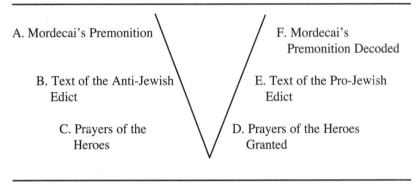

A. Mordecai's Premonition

B. Text of the Anti-Jewish
   Edict

C. Prayers of the
   Heroes

F. Mordecai's
   Premonition Decoded

E. Text of the Pro-Jewish
   Edict

D. Prayers of the Heroes
   Granted

FIGURE 3

The symmetry is, again, not perfect, since chap. D does not yet represent the granting of all that is asked in chap. C. One might note as well that the effect of the juxtaposition of chaps. C and D is to make the point between them the pivotal moment, at the expense of chap. 6.[51]

Whereas the interpolation of the six Greek texts does not significantly change the structure of the Masoretic book of Esther, it does give the *megillah* a rather different cast. As Clines observes, "the primary effect of the LXX expansions as a whole is . . . to *assimilate the book of Esther to a scriptural norm,* especially as found in Ezra, Nehemiah, and Daniel." For example, as in the "Persian histories of Ezra and Nehemiah" (e.g., Ezra 1:1, 5; 6:22; Neh. 2:8, 12, 20), the "explicit language of divine causation [appears in] only a few, though critical, interventions of God in the historical process" (e.g., D:8 and F:6). It bears attention that this explicit mention of God, so different from the MT, also appears in the LXX in passages that do have MT equivalents. For example, whereas in 6:1 we read in the MT, "sleep eluded the King," the LXX reads "the LORD kept sleep away from the King."[52] This, too, represents an assimilation of the book to a scriptural norm, though there is room to wonder, as we shall see, whether it is not the MT that is actually innovating here and the LXX that is holding fast to a more original, and explicitly theological, telling of the tale.

Chapters B and E, the texts of the anti-Jewish and pro-Jewish edicts, re-

[51]See above, pp. 6–7.
[52]Clines, 169–70.

spectively, recall a number of biblical passages that purport to be the texts of the decrees or confessions of faith of foreign emperors or the letters of anti-Jewish elements about to be overruled (e.g., Ezra 1:2–4; 4:7–22; Dan. 3:31–4:34; cf. 3 Macc. 3:12–29).[53] These two interpolations enhance the annalistic nature of the MT's style and lend more credibility to the tale, or at least attempt to do so.

The stirring and eloquent prayers in chap. C lay to rest suspicions of unorthodox behavior to which the MT can give rise—for example, that Mordecai's refusal to bow to Haman was not religiously motivated or that Esther enjoyed being married to a Gentile and eating non-kosher food.[54] In so doing, chap. C assimilates Esther to the scriptural norm defined by Pentateuchal law, the observance of which is central to the Judaism of the Second Temple as well as all succeeding periods. In addition, as Clines points out, "[t]hese prayers assist in remolding the book into the form of an *exemplary* tale—which does not only record divine deliverance or divine-human cooperation but also gives advice on how Jews should behave religiously in a foreign environment or a situation of crisis."[55] As he notes, prayers of supplication of this sort are common in Second Temple Judaism (e.g., Ezra 9:6–15; Neh. 1:5–11; 9:6–37; Dan. 9:4–19; Judith 9).

Finally, the premonitory dream of Mordecai in chap. A and its decoding in chap. F assimilate the MT Book of Esther to the emerging scriptural tradition of apocalyptic literature. The story is transformed into the manifestation in human history of a cosmic conflict between God and the demonic forces that oppose him and afflict his chosen people. Clines argues that "the effect of superimposing this framework upon the Greek book of Esther . . . is to conform it more closely to scriptural precedent in the book of Daniel," where "the *meaning* of history is conveyed through dreams and their interpretation" (e.g., Daniel 2; cf. the visions of chaps. 7–12).[56] This is probably too specific. Since the Septuagintal Esther shows no signs of influence from Daniel itself, it is better to assume a parallel rather than influence: in both instances, old tales of Jews in foreign courts have been recontextualized within an apocalyptic milieu.

Although the ongoing Jewish tradition lost these six "Additions to Esther" and does not deem them canonical, they are still valuable witnesses to the nature of Judaism late in the Second Temple period and thus are important to Jewish history and to the background of Christianity as well. Exactly when they

[53]Ibid., 173–74.

[54]Note that the LXX to 2:7 has Mordecai raising Esther to be a wife (*eis gynaika*) rather than a daughter, as in the MT. This is probably the earliest attestation of the Jewish tradition that Mordecai and Esther were actually married, first explicitly enunciated in the name of Rabbi Meir, a Tanna of the second century C.E. (*b. Meg.* 13a).

[55]Clines, 171.

[56]Ibid., 171–72.

were composed is again difficult to specify. The apologetic or apocalyptic tendencies of most of them recommend the second century B.C.E.

One particular Greek manuscript tradition merits special attention because it offers evidence not only about the post-MT evolution of the tale of Esther and Mordecai, as do the LXX manuscripts, but also, and uniquely, about the shape of the story—or *one* shape of the story—before the MT revised it. The Alpha Text (AT) contains a stratum that recounts the tale in ways that are different from both the MT and the LXX and cannot be derived from either of those closely related textual traditions.[57] Indeed, meticulous analysis of this AT stratum, which Fox calls the "proto-AT," confirms it to be the Greek translation of a Hebrew original that was shorter and earlier than the MT and different from it in several highly significant ways.[58] For example, the story of the conspiracy of the two eunuchs against the king, which appears in the MT and the LXX as 2:21–23 and in the LXX alone as A:13–17 as well, is missing altogether from the proto-AT. Clines argues that this vignette is a midrashic expansion of a vague allusion in the AT to "a conspiracy of the eunuchs and a benefit which Mordecai had rendered the king" (AT 7:3, corresponding chronologically to MT 6:1–3).[59] The double appearance of this story in the LXX suggests that chap. A is presupposing a form of the story other than the MT—that is, a form in which 2:21–23 did not already exist. Otherwise, it is difficult to understand why the author of the new opening chapter would both transfer the story (with some changes) to the beginning of the tale and leave it where he found it at the end of chap. 2. The most reasonable conclusion is that A:13–17 and 2:21–23 testify to two related but variant attempts to introduce a new passage into the Esther tradition. And, in fact, the AT alone offers compelling evidence for the newness of the little story of the two disloyal eunuchs.

Possessed of canonical status in no surviving tradition, the AT is nonetheless invaluable for the light it sheds on the prehistory of the two canonical versions of the book of Esther, the MT and the LXX. In order to understand how the MT shaped the earlier tradition, it is worthwhile to mention other salient divergences. The first of these is the absence in the AT of any assumption of the irrevocability of Persian law. This is, as we have mentioned, an assumption lacking in the extrabiblical sources as well but present in the book of Daniel (Dan. 6:9, 13, 16). By introducing the notion that Persian imperial decrees can never be revoked, the MT (or one of its immediate ancestors) added

---

[57]See Carey A. Moore, "A Greek Witness to a Different Text of Esther," *ZAW* 79 (1967): 351–58; rpt. in Moore, *Studies,* 521–28. The AT is reprinted in Clines, 216–47, and in Fox, *Redaction,* 157–67. Clines includes an English translation.

[58]Clines, 71–94; Fox, *Redaction,* 17–34.

[59]Clines, 104–107.

enormous excitement to the end of the tale, for now we must reckon not just with the dispatch of the enemies of the Jews, but rather with a gory clash of two irrevocable edicts, one against Jews and one against anti-Semites (3:12–15; 8:9–14).[60] Since both have been issued by the highest known human authority, we see here the comical self-contradiction of Ahasuerus's regime and detect as well, in the total victory of the Jews, the hand of a higher authority than he.

The second salient innovation of the MT (or one of its immediate ancestors) is the transformation of the story into an etiology of Purim, which is unmentioned in the AT book of Esther.[61] This adds potent fuel to the speculation that Purim began as a non-Jewish festival and was only secondarily associated with the great victory over anti-Semitism in the days of Esther and Mordecai. For the AT demonstrates the converse—that the tale of Esther and Mordecai once existed independently of the holiday for which it has become the festal legend.

The last change introduced by the MT (or a text or tradition from which it is derived) is the removal of all explicit references to God or the gods. In this, it is distinct from both the AT and the LXX, in which explicit mention of the Deity is amply attested. For example, whereas the AT shows Haman casting lots in order to consult "his gods to learn the day of [the Jews'] death" (AT 4:7), the MT narrates the lot-taking without reference to its instigator's religious purposes (3:7). Even more interesting is a comparison of Mordecai's warning to Esther when she flinches from her great assignment. Where the AT reads, "God will be their help (*boēthos*) and deliverance" (AT 5:9), the MT reads "relief [LXX, *boētheia*] and deliverance will arise for the Jews from another quarter" (4:14). Though the direction of development in this and the other cases is not indisputably clear, Clines is probably correct that "the MT represents a deliberate excision of *all* religious language," i.e., pagan as well as Jewish.[62] The reason for the change would seem to be the MT's adherence to a subtle and demanding theology in which religious meaning is not manifest in human actions but lies behind them (see above, pp. 17–21).

Even the proto-AT almost certainly had antecedents, oral or written, but to reconstruct them would be not only speculative in the extreme but a diversion from our task of introducing the surviving versions of the book of Esther.[63]

---

[60]See Fox, *Redaction,* 38–39, against Clines, 74–84.

[61]But note AT 8:34, where Mordecai enjoins the Jews "to have a celebration unto God." There is no indication that this is Purim, however, or that it is to take place on Adar 14 or 15.

[62]See Clines, 109.

[63]See Henri Cazelles, "Note sur la composition du rouleau d'Esther," in *Lex tua veritas,* ed. H. Gross and F. Mussner, Trier, 1961, 17–29; Clines, 115–38; and Lawrence M. Wills, *The Jew in the Court of the Foreign King,* HDR, Minneapolis, 1990, 153–91; J. T. Milik, "Les Modèles araméens du livre d'Esther dans la grotte 4 de Qumrân," *RQ* 15 (1992): 321–99.

Figure 4, a diagram of the redactional history of the book, adapted from Fox,[64] is most helpful. In it, Proto-Esther refers to those unrecoverable sources, and "R" stands for "redactor."

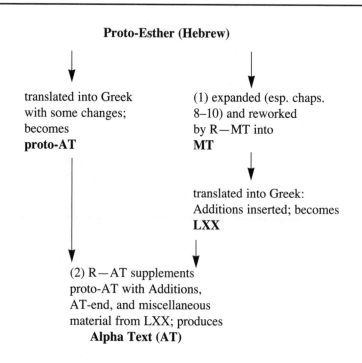

FIGURE 4

[64]Fox, *Redaction*, 9; *Character*, 255. A Greek translation of the MT also seems to have come into existence at some point. See Horace G. Lunt and Moshe Taube, "The Slavonic Book of Esther: Translation from Hebrew or Evidence for a Lost Greek Text?" *HTR* 87 (1994): 347–62.

ESTHER

Mordecai's Premonition

Chapter A:1–17 (= Esther 11:2–12:6 in the Vulgate)

A:1 *In the second year of the reign of Artaxerxes the Great, on the first of Nisan, Mordecai, son of Jair, son of Shimei, son of Kish, of the tribe of Benjamin, had a dream.* 2 *He was a Jewish man residing in the city of Susa, an important man serving at the king's court.* 3 *But he was also one of the captives whom Nebuchadnezzar, the king of Babylon, had taken from Jerusalem, with Jeconiah, the king of Judah.*

4 *This was his dream: There was noise, clamor, thunder, and earthquake—tumult upon the earth.* 5 *Then two enormous dragons came forth, both readied for combat. A mighty cry came from them,* 6 *and at their cry every people readied itself for war in order to fight against the race of the righteous.* 7 *It was a day of darkness and gloom; oppression and distress, evil and disorder lay upon the earth.* 8 *Then the entire race of the just were dismayed, terrified of the evils awaiting them, and they prepared themselves to be destroyed and cried out to God.* 9 *And as they cried out, a great river, vast waters, issued, as it were, from a small spring.* 10 *The light of the sun broke forth. The lowly were exalted and devoured the people of high repute.*

11 *Having had this dream and seen what God had planned to do, Mordecai awoke. He kept the dream in mind and continually sought to discover its meaning, until nightfall.*

12 *When Mordecai was resting at the court with Gabatha and Tharra, the two eunuchs of the king who guarded the court,* 13 *he heard them in a discussion, and investigating what was on their minds, he learned that they were preparing to lay hands upon King Artaxerxes. So he informed the king about them,* 14 *and the king had the two interrogated. When they confessed, they were carried off.* 15 *Then the king had these things written down as a matter of record; Mordecai also put them into writing.* 16 *The king appointed Mordecai to serve at court and gave him rewards for his deeds.*

17 *But Haman, son of Hammedatha, a Bugaean, a man in high repute with the king, sought to do harm to Mordecai and his people on account of the two eunuchs of the king.*

Chapter A introduces one of the heroes of the tale (vv. 1–3), tells of a dream of his that foreshadows the crucial action of the subsequent narrative in a highly symbolic way (vv. 4–11), and closes with an account of his reward by the king for having exposed an assassination plot on the part of two courtiers (vv. 12–17). On the nature of the chapters in Esther indicated by letters rather than numbers, see the Introduction, section 5.

The identification of Mordecai in A:1–3 repeats the gist of Esth. 2:5–6. Since the latter text introduces Mordecai rather completely, with a three-generation genealogy, a tribal affiliation, and an account of how he was forced to leave Jerusalem, it is highly unlikely that it knew of the prior report of the identical material in chap. A. The identification of the Persian king as Artaxerxes is normal in the LXX and stands in contrast to the "Ahasuerus" of the MT and several other ancient versions (which the Greeks rendered as "Xerxes"). The commencement of the narrative in the king's second regnal year (A:1) places the dream and the elevation of Mordecai a year ahead of the beginning of events in the Masoretic Text (1:3). The date of the dream, the first of the month of Nisan, marks the spring New Year's Day (as opposed to the fall New Year's Day, now known as Rosh Hashanah), since Nisan is counted as the first month of the year in Jewish calendars of the Second Temple period. In the Torah, this day had already come to be associated with two happy events: the drying up of the lethal waters from the earth in the time of Noah (Gen. 8:13) and the establishment of the Tabernacle in the time of Moses (Exod. 40:2, 17). In Esther A, the spring New Year is associated with two other happy events, a revelatory dream of the rescue of the Jewish race from a lethal threat and the establishment of Mordecai in the king's court. Perhaps one is also to detect here an echo of the Babylonian and later Jewish idea that the destinies for the coming year were assigned on New Year's Day.

In one important respect, the introduction of Mordecai in A:1–3 differs from the parallel in 2:5–6. The latter text (which is chronologically earlier) closes with the essential information that Mordecai had adopted his orphaned cousin, the highly attractive Hadassah, as she is known in Hebrew, or Esther, as she appears in the rest of the book (2:7). Addition A is noteworthy for its lack of direct mention of Esther, to whom allusion is made only in the highly symbolic form of the "small spring" that becomes "a great river" in A:9. In the MT, by way of contrast, Mordecai and Esther share the role of hero and chief protagonist. It is he who passes to her the news of the genocide decreed against the Jews and who finally persuades her to approach the king on behalf of her beleaguered people (chap. 4), and it is he who is rewarded with promotion to the rank of second-in-command of the Persian empire, the highest rank to which a Jew, even with a substantial stretch of the imagination, could aspire. It is on this note of the glorification of Mordecai that the MT closes the tale (10:2–3). Yet it is Esther who risks her very life in carrying out her foster father's stratagem (4:16), which she does with considerable rhetorical skill (5:1–8; 7:1–6), and she, to all appearances, remains queen even after the anti-Semitic conspirators have been eliminated. Given the joint heroism of Mordecai and Esther, it is appropriate that both of them issue letters enjoining the observance of Purim, the holiday that commemorates the events in the book of Esther (9:20–32).

It is not only in the omission of all mention of Hadassah/Esther in the introduction in vv. 1–3 that chap. A increases the emphasis upon Mordecai. The same development can be seen in the account of the foiling of the assassins' plot in vv. 12–15. Here we are told that "he informed the king about them" (v. 13), whereas in the Masoretic parallel (2:21–23), he "disclosed it to Queen Esther, and Esther told it to the king in Mordecai's name" (v. 22). It is doubtful that the change results from a deliberate decision to downplay the heroine or from greater androcentrism on the part of the author of chap. A. Certainly Esther's role is not generally minimized in the Additions; in fact, in chaps. C and D her courage, religiousness, and eloquence are developed far beyond anything in the MT. It seems that in the post-Masoretic growth of the Esther narrative, the characteristic heroism of both protagonists has been greatly enhanced, but that Mordecai's status as the successful Jewish courtier has led to some shift in the distribution of roles. Note, for example, that A:2 presents him from the start as "an important man serving at the king's court," another idea missing in the Masoretic parallel in 2:5–6. Another testimony to the pride with which some segments of Judaism in the Second Temple period viewed Mordecai is the name given to Purim in 2 Macc. 15:36, "the Day of Mordecai."

Mordecai's allegorical dream, related in A:4–10, is decoded in the closing "Addition," F:1–6. The two dragons are Mordecai and Haman; "every people" is the anti-Semites; "the race of the just" is the Jews; "the great river [that] issued, as it were, from a small spring" is Esther. Both the dream itself and the decoding of it after the narrative has run its course, however, have their problems. The image of the dragons in combat derives from ancient Near Eastern creation myths in which a sea monster personifies chaos and poses a challenge to the creator-god (cf. Isa. 51:9–11; Ps. 74:12–17). But it cannot be established that the "dragons" in Esth. A:4–10 are aquatic, and the account of *two* of them, fighting not with God but with each other, is atypical. This latter problem can be mitigated somewhat by reference to the later development of rabbinic eschatological speculations in which two monsters, Leviathan and Behemoth, attack each other.[65] Though Mordecai's dream appears to be an earlier form of this mythological motif, the problem remains that in the decoding of chap. F, not only the demonic opponent of God's reign but also the hero, Mordecai, is represented as a mighty beast. It is also odd that both beasts—not only Haman,

[65]E.g., see *PRK* 188b (Buber ed.). See Levenson, *Creation,* 34–46.

but also Mordecai in the interpretation of chap. F—utter the "mighty cry" that signals to the anti-Semites (here described as "every people," as is not the case in the MT story of Esther) to ready themselves to destroy the Jews (A:5–6). And one element that one would surely expect in an adaptation of the ancient combat myth is strangely missing here—the destruction of the evil beast. Perhaps it is to be assumed from the report that "the lowly . . . devoured the people of high repute" (A:10). Even if this be so, the allusion is oddly indirect and lacking in vividness.

The effect of Mordecai's dream in A:4–9 and its interpretation in F:1–6 is to bracket the book of Esther within a structure of prophecy and fulfillment, a well-known biblical pattern (e.g., 2 Kings 6:33–7:20). The essential events now appear as foreordained, at least to those who, like Mordecai, are graced with revelation and have the faith to persevere to the end despite the opacity of the revelation. These two Additions are thus, in part, early interpretations of the story of Esther. They resolve a question that the MT leaves suggestively open: Whence came the happy ending to what might have been a gruesome story of genocide and anti-Semitism triumphant? The help came from God, the Additions tell us, to whom the people cried out (A:8) and who was, despite appearances, always completely in control, from even before Haman hatched his foul plot to obliterate the Jews (F:1). This uninhibited attribution of the deliverance of the Jewish people to God conforms not only to the general biblical pattern, but also to the way the Jewish tradition has historically interpreted Esther. It does not, however, conform to the book itself in the MT, which never mentions the name of God and is noteworthy in its lack of theological editorializing. Like the Additions to Esther in general, and like the history of Esther's reception within the Jewish tradition, Mordecai's dream moves the book away from its subtle, ambiguous, and naturalistic "theology" (if the word is appropriate at all) and toward a more conventional stance of simple, robust piety.

The highly symbolic character of the dream itself and the element of predetermination that it injects represent something more than the prophecy–fulfillment schema of classical biblical historiography. They have strong affinities with Jewish and early Christian apocalyptic literature, in which combat with fearsome beasts and the miraculous rescue of the righteous minority after horrific afflictions are major themes (e.g., Daniel 7 and Revelation 12). Both the occurrence of Mordecai's premonitory dream and its content recall the book of Daniel in particular and suggest that chap. A may have come from the same period as the apocalyptic visions in Daniel, that is, the second century B.C.E. The bracketing of the older parts of the book of Esther within the framework of chaps. A and F results from a recontextualization in an apocalyptic mode somewhat reminiscent of the reconception of the court sage Daniel as an apocalyptic seer.

Esther A:11 represents a transition from Mordecai's premonitory dream to the beginning of its implementation in his overhearing the assassination plot of the two courtiers. According to vv. 11–12, his discovery of the conspiracy occurred on the very next night after the revelation of God's plan in the dream. This chronology stands in sharp contrast to the MT, in which Mordecai's discovery of the plot occurs only after Esther has been chosen queen and thus long after the onset of the narrative. One should also note that whereas in the MT the king rewards Mordecai for saving his life only much later (6:1–11), here he rewards him immediately. The names of the two conspirators in Addition A, Gabatha and Tharra (v. 12) also differ from the names in the MT, Bigthan(a) and Teresh (2:21; 6:2), though not drastically. The differences in chronology and nomenclature suggest the important point that Addition A is something other than a mere augmentation of the story of Esther known to us from the MT. Rather, it seems to derive from a variant telling of the core Esther story. The precise shape of that variant cannot be determined because only fragments of it survive. What we actually have in the longer, LXX version of the book of Esther, in other words, is the combination of more than one form of the Esther tradition. As we shall see, this may also be true of the shorter, MT version as well.

The concluding verse of Addition A represents yet another variation from the MT. Whereas the latter attributes Haman's desire to harm Mordecai to rage over the Jewish courtier's failure to bow down to him (3:5–6), the Addition associates Haman with the conspiracy of the two eunuchs that Mordecai has just foiled. The effect is to make Haman not only the "enemy of the Jews" (8:1) but also the enemy of the Persian king, that is, an antisocial person in general. The mysterious term "Bugaean," applied to Haman in A:17 (cf. 3:1), if it is not simply a scribal mistake, probably had a derogatory connotation that added to this impression. Perhaps we are to understand that the two eunuchs were conspiring to replace King Artaxerxes with Haman. If so, then A:17 builds on the impression given in 6:6–9 that Haman covets the royal office, for there he tries to persuade Ahasuerus to let him be paraded through the city in the king's own garb and on the king's own horse. The same impression of insurrection comes into Ahasuerus's own mind in 7:8, when, seeing Haman "falling onto the couch upon which Esther reclined," the king mistakes this gesture of supplication for a sexual assault. Since a move upon the reigning monarch's harem can signal that a rebellion is under way (as in 2 Sam. 16:20–22 and 1 Kings 2:19–25), it would seem that the king's misimpression (if such it be) is based upon more than sexual possessiveness. By associating Haman with the failed conspiracy of the two eunuchs, A:17 makes explicit what is only implied (and none too clearly) in 6:6–9 and 7:8. It also suggests a reason for Mordecai's enigmatic refusal to bow down to Haman in 3:1–5—Mordecai will show no deference to a potential regicide. This portrayal of Haman as a traitor to the Persian emperor does not mesh well with the apocalyptic image in A:6, in which "every people

readied itself for war in order to fight against the race of the righteous." It is
likely that the apocalyptic vision in Mordecai's dream comes from a different
traditionary circle from that responsible for the depiction of Haman as someone in league with the two eunuchs.

I. A New Queen Is Chosen

Esther 1:1–2:20

1. Three Royal Banquets (1:1–9)

1:1 These events occurred in the days of Ahasuerus—the same Ahasuerus
who reigned from India to Nubia, a hundred twenty-seven provinces.
2 In those days, when King Ahasuerus sat upon his royal throne in the
fortified compound of Susa, **3** in the third year of his reign, he gave a banquet for all his officials and his courtiers, with the military commanders[a]
of Persia and Media, the noblemen, and the governors of the provinces
in attendance, **4** displaying the vast wealth of his kingdom and the resplendent glory of his majesty for a long period, a hundred and eighty
days. **5** When these days[b] were over, the king gave a banquet of seven
days' duration for all the men[c] present in the fortified compound of Susa,
high and low alike, in the courtyard of the royal pavilion. **6** There were
curtains of white cotton and violet wool fastened by cords of fine linen
and purple wool to silver rods and marble pillars. There were couches of
gold and silver on a mosaic pavement of porphyry, marble, mother-of-
pearl, and other precious stones.[d] **7** The drinks were served in gold cups
of all different designs[e]—vast amounts of royal wine, as befitted the
king's liberality. **8** And the drinking was according to the law: there was
no compulsion, for the king had ordered every steward of his palace to
respect each man's wishes. **9** In addition, Queen Vashti gave a banquet
for the women in the royal palace of King Ahasuerus.

a. It is possible that *ḥêl* refers to the powerful people of the imperial government
itemized throughout the verse, or simply to the army collectively. Our translation inserts *wĕśārê* ("officers, commanders, rulers") before it, which may have fallen out when
a scribe failed to note that the term occurs twice in the verse. The LXX reads "his
friends" in place of "all his officials and his courtiers" but then inserts "and for all the
other nations." Behind the words "and all the other" (*kai tois loipois*), some scholars
have suspected a misreading or miscopying of Heb. *wśry* as *wš'r,* but this still leaves
the reference to "nations" unexplained.
b. The LXX reads "the days of the wedding (or, wedding-feast)" which, though it

explains much (see the commentary), may be an exegetical gloss rather than an authentic reading.

c. *hā'ām* is rendered "men" rather than "people" because the women would presumably have attended Vashti's alternative party (1:9).

d. The names of fabrics and stones in this verse are difficult to identify. The author may be employing exotic terms to enhance the sense of extreme opulence.

e. The meaning of *wĕkēlîm mikkēlîm šônîm* is unclear. If the reference is not to different types of gold cups, then perhaps we are to think that no one drank from the same cup twice.

The shorter, or Masoretic, version of the book of Esther opens with an identification of the king in whose reign the events take place. The name "Ahasuerus" is the Hebrew form of the Persian name that the Greeks rendered as "Xerxes." The gloss that is Esth. 1:1b is perhaps intended to differentiate this emperor from another man of the same name. Note, for example, the "Ahasuerus" who is Darius's father in Dan. 9:1, perhaps the same man who is identified in Ezra 4:6 as an emperor who ruled between Cyrus and Darius. The historical evidence, however, does not support the existence of any Ahasuerus before the reign of Darius I. The king in the Masoretic book of Esther is probably meant to be identified with Xerxes I, who reigned from 486–465 B.C.E. The hundred twenty-seven provinces of Esth. 1:1 is also historically unlikely. Why provinces rather than satrapies are mentioned is unclear: 3:12 indicates that the two divisions were not identical. Even applied to some smaller unit than the satrapy, however, the number does not correspond with anything known from the Persian imperial structure. It has been suggested that it might be symbolic, perhaps derived from the product of twelve for the tribes of Israel and ten as a common expression of completeness, with seven added on to express perfection.[66] Twelve, ten, and seven are all indeed significant numbers in the Bible, and one can fruitfully compare the one hundred twenty-seven provinces with the one hundred twenty years of maximum longevity in Gen. 6:3 (also the lifespan of Moses in Deut. 34:7) as well as with the many sets of seven in the Bible, including sets of seven years (e.g., Exod. 21:2 and Lev. 25:8). In this respect, it is interesting to note that Gen. 23:1 gives the same figure for Sarah's years of life as the book of Esther gives for the number of provinces under Ahasuerus's control, one hundred twenty-seven.

The multiple difficulties in squaring the historical information in Esther with the evidence from ancient historiography and the presence in the book of symbolic figures suggest that Esther is seriously misinterpreted if it is taken as literal historical reportage. The historical information in it is, in fact, rather incidental to the action of the narrative, and much of the author's artistry and

[66]Paton, 124.

message will be missed if factually accurate historiography is seen as the intention. The historical improbability of the book is a point that will appear repeatedly in our reading of it. It is best to become aware at the outset that an honest recognition of this issue need imply no impairment of the religious or literary worth of the book.

Why the text tells us that the initial events occurred "when King Ahasuerus sat upon his royal throne in Susa" (Esth. 1:2) is unclear. Since the action occurs "in the third year of his reign" (1:3), the reference cannot be to his enthronement. The rabbinic tradition may be correct that the clause refers to the point when he secured his reign after a two-year period of political unsettlement.[67] Others have suggested that the key word is "Susa" and that the point is to distinguish this from other royal residences for which there is evidence.[68] Given the importance of Susa throughout the book, this latter suggestion seems the better one, though it should be noted that the Greek historian Herodotus (7:7), in a parallel to the rabbinic interpretation, tells us that Xerxes subdued Egypt only in his second year, that is, just before the action of the Masoretic Esther commences. The word *bîrâ*, rendered above as "fortified compound," (Esth. 1:2), refers to the "royal part of the capital which is separated from the city."[69] A distinction must evidently be made between this area and the city of Susa itself (see 3:15; 6:11; 9:11–15).

The action gets under way with Ahasuerus's banquet in his third regnal year (1:3). If we correlate this date with extrabiblical chronology and assume that Ahasuerus shares not just the name but also the identity of Xerxes I, we must date the onset of the narrative to 483 B.C.E. It is surely no coincidence that the action of the book both begins and ends with banqueting (cf. 9:19, 22). Bardtke astutely points out that the opening three feasts celebrate Persian wealth and power (1:3–9), whereas the closing feast, the original Purim, celebrates Jewish deliverance and survival.[70] We can go further. The turning point of the book is also a matter of feasts—the two banquets in which the Persian king and his Jewish queen sup together (5:6–8 and 7:1–9)—and it is in only the second of these (7:1–9) that the crucial transition is made from Persian power to Jewish deliverance. It is worth noting that whereas Persian power ended with Alexander the Great's conquest of the empire in the fourth century B.C.E., Jewish deliverance, though often in doubt, continues to be celebrated even now in the yearly feast of Purim.

The description of the feast in 1:3–4 is probably continued in v. 6; v. 5, which speaks of a subsequent banquet, seems to be an interruption.[71] The de-

---

[67]See *b. Meg.* 11b and Rashi to Esth. 1:2.

[68]Paton, 125.

[69]Moore, *Esther*, 5.

[70]Hans Bardtke, *Das Buch Esther,* KAT, Gütersloh, 1963, 276 (hereafter this book will be identified as "Bardtke").

[71]See Ibn Ezra to Esth. 1:6.

scription goes to great lengths to stress the opulence of the king's affair, listing not only the various classes of distinguished invitees but also the fabrics adorning the pillars of the palace, the precious metals in the couches, and the gems in the pavement. The precise identification of some of these materials is uncertain. Harder to believe is the length of the first banquet, one hundred eighty days, and the presence at it of *all* the noblemen and military commanders in the empire. To be sure, analogies, ancient and modern, have been cited: for example, the one-hundred-twenty-day festival in Judith 1:16 or the Assyrian emperor Assurnasirpal's feast with 69,574 guests.[72] But the historicity of these analogies is also open to doubt, and it is impossible to imagine that the affairs of a political entity as complex as the Persian empire could have been conducted for long in the absence of so many essential officers. Who was minding the store during this drinkfest of half a year's duration?

The description of the banquets in this first paragraph is, thus, less historical than hyperbolic. The point is to stress the overwhelming wealth, power, and status of the king of Persia, for these are what the Jews, soon to be condemned to genocide, will have to overcome. Their victory, in short, will go against all odds. The banquets also speak to the moral status of the king who sponsors them. To say that he is ostentatious is to engage in gross understatement. The narrative is, in fact, so focused on the external trappings that it leaves the perspicacious reader wondering what the internal life of Ahasuerus can be like. On this, there is not a word, but contextualized within the moral universe of the Hebrew Bible, especially its wisdom literature, this enormous emphasis on wealth and status cannot speak well for the man who holds the world's most powerful office. "In time of trouble," the psalmist proclaims, "why should I fear / . . . men who trust in their riches, / who glory in their great wealth? . . . Man does not abide in honor; he is like the beasts that perish" (Ps. 49:6–7, 13). Wealth and glory are very much at the center of this narrative and Ahasuerus's mind as well, but the limitations of his sybaritic mode of life will soon become painfully evident. Some of the language of 1:4 will recur in 5:11, when Haman boasts to his wife and friends about his own wealth and power—just before having to accept the humiliating office of herald to Mordecai (chap. 6). "Pride goes before ruin, / Arrogance, before failure" (Prov. 16:18). In the end, Haman's assets will be assigned to Esther and Mordecai (Esth. 8:7), and it is the Jew Mordecai who appears in public clad in the lavish robes of royalty. The verse that tells us this (8:15) has some verbal affinities with the description of the appointments of the banquet hall in 1:6. Part of the moral message of the book of Esther is that wealth flows to those who place other things at the center of their lives, to those who are discreet, not ostentatious, and tight-lipped rather than given to braggadocio.

[72]Bardtke, 279.

The reason for the banquet is not given. One can speculate that it was in honor of securing the king's throne at last or of moving his royal residence to Susa from elsewhere. The LXX to 1:5 suggests another possibility: it was to celebrate his marriage to Vashti. If we are to think of a wedding feast, then the second banquet, of seven days' duration and for the benefit only of those within the fortified compound (v. 5), would be the more reasonable candidate. (Note that feasting for a week after the nuptials is an ancient Jewish practice [cf. Gen. 29:27–28], still observed today.) If so, then an analogy with "the banquet of Esther" that Ahasuerus gives after crowning her queen (2:18) may be in order; for that, too, may have been a wedding feast rather than a coronation banquet. If 1:5 does speak of wedding festivities, then the king's decision to order Queen Vashti to appear "wearing a royal diadem in order to show her beauty to the peoples and the officers" (1:11) is less abrupt than otherwise seems the case.

The description of the drinking in 1:7–8 does not elevate our estimation of Ahasuerus's character or of the moral fiber of the Persian aristocracy in general. Verse 8 seems to say that "the law" (*dāt*) was that there should be no law: everyone could drink as much as he wanted. As Fox nicely puts it, "this king tends to let people do as they want."[73] The same permissiveness and lack of standards will be evident when the king approves Haman's petition to annihilate the Jews, handing him his signet ring without so much as a word of interrogation or a moment of deliberation (3:9–11). Significantly, the order of genocide is also called "law," and its promulgation is followed by the king and Haman's sitting down to drink (3:15). Fortunately, Ahasuerus's malleability and his inability to say no will also work for the salvation of the Jewish people once Esther has made her case (7:9b; chap. 8), which once again results in the proclamation of a "law" (or "decree," *dāt;* 8:13). But nothing happens in this tale to dissipate our initial impression that Ahasuerus is a spoiled playboy, a person who overindulges in physical pleasures and lacks a moral compass. Fortunately for the Jews and for him as well, a felicitous sequence of coincidences, together with some shrewd planning and gutsiness on the part of Mordecai and Esther, allows them to fill the void that stands where his conscience and prudence should have been.

Why Queen Vashti gives a banquet for the women (1:9) is a bit puzzling. Elsewhere in the book and in Herodotus (5:18), we find women partying with the men at Persian banquets. Whatever its historical unlikelihood, Esth. 1:9 does fill some important narrative functions. The absence of women at Ahasuerus's banquets enhances the perception that these were really just overdone "stag parties," with all the licentiousness and disrespect the term implies. The absence of Vashti from her husband's banquet sets the stage for the pivotal mo-

---

[73]Fox, *Character,* 17.

ment in which she refuses his command to appear (1:10–12). And her presence at her own party emphasizes the separation, perhaps even the incommensurability, of the worlds of the king and of the queen—a theme that will continue long after Vashti has been deposed and the Jewess Esther has replaced her.

2. Vashti's Refusal (1:10–12)

1:10 On the seventh day, when the king was merry with wine, he ordered Mehuman, Bizzetha, Harbona, Bigtha, Abagtha, Zethar, and Carcas, the seven eunuchs in attendance upon the person of King Ahasuerus, 11 to bring Queen Vashti into the presence of the king wearing a royal diadem in order to show her beauty to the peoples and the officers, for she was indeed a beautiful woman. 12 But Queen Vashti refused to come at the king's command, conveyed by the eunuchs. The king became highly incensed, and his rage burned within him.

Having shown off his wealth and his power, Ahasuerus now seeks to show off his wife, as if she is in the same category. That he seeks to do so when he is "merry with wine" (*kĕṭôb lēb hammelek bayyāyin*, 1:10) does not augur well. "Wine is not for kings," a royal mother admonishes her son in Prov. 31:4, and a number of biblical narratives with close affinities to ours bear this out. The most analogous situation occurs in Daniel 5, when King Balshazzar, during a banquet for his thousand noblemen and "[u]nder the influence of the wine," orders the gold and silver vessels captured from the Temple at Jerusalem brought out and used for drink (v. 2). In response to this rank sacrilege, mysterious handwriting appears on the wall, which Daniel decodes as predicting Belshazzar's loss of his empire to the Medes and the Persians. Several close verbal analogies to Esth. 1:10 underscore this connection between intoxication and impending doom. For example, "Nabal was in a merry mood (*wĕlēb nābāl ṭôb 'ālāyw*) and very drunk" (1 Sam. 25:36) just before his wife, Abigail, tells him of her solicitude for David, God strikes him dead, and David marries his widow. Similarly, Amnon is "merry with wine" (*kĕṭôb lēb 'amnôn bayyayin*, 2 Sam. 13:28) when he is struck dead at Absalom's command. Similar language (though without direct reference to liquor) occurs in Esth. 5:9, when "Haman went out [from the queen's wine feast] that day joyful and merry" (*śāmēaḥ wĕṭôb lēb*) only to become enraged at the sight of Mordecai, who will soon be his downfall.

There are other parallels between Ahasuerus and Haman, even in this passage. The king's crass desire to show off his wife's beauty recalls Haman's wish to show off his closeness to the king in 6:7–9—once again with quite the opposite result (Haman's appointment as herald to his nemesis Mordecai [vv. 10–11]). Moreover, Queen Vashti's refusal to come to Ahasuerus's party, resulting in the king's intense rage (1:12), is reminiscent of Mordecai's refusal to bow down to Haman, who is then "filled with rage" (3:5). In the cases of both Vashti and Mordecai, no reason for the refusal is given, though (especially in her case) it is not hard to think of good possibilities.[74] The two instances have another commonality in that both result in a deposition, Vashti's own and Haman's. The narrative analogy is this: Vashti : Ahasuerus :: Mordecai : Haman.

There are, however, some revealing contrasts that complicate the multifaceted analogy between Haman and Ahasuerus. Whereas the former dies an ignominious death, the latter remains on his throne and thrives (chap. 10). Haman's is an active evil, directed against the Jews, a people who benefit from a mysterious protection (6:13), whereas Ahasuerus is only a weak, passive, and unfocused person, who can be and is persuaded to come to the Jews' defense.

There are other complications in the fourfold analogy of principal characters as well. Whereas Vashti loses an office, Mordecai gains one. And Vashti is paired not only with Mordecai in an unexplained refusal to oblige a superior; she is also paired with Esther, but in a contrastive fashion. Whereas Vashti's courage lies in her refusal to come before the king at his bidding, Esther's is shown in her willingness (not without initial hesitation, 4:10–14) to approach the king unbidden (4:15–5:1). These opposing manifestations of courage also bring about opposing results. Whereas Vashti is dethroned and never heard from again (perhaps we are to think she was executed), Esther remains on the throne and secures life for her condemned people.

Although plausible Persian etymologies have been proposed for the name "Vashti," there is no extrabiblical evidence for a queen with that name. According to Herodotus (9:109–12), Xerxes's wife's name was Amestris. Commentaries often cite the Greek legend of the Lydian Gyges[75] as an analogy to the story of Vashti, but the similarity is scant and influence is unlikely. It is hard not to sympathize with Vashti when her loutish husband orders her to appear before his drinking companions in order to display her physical attraction, and some may wish to make of her a feminist heroine. The narrator, however, has no interest in her after this brief passage. Queen Vashti's absolute and uncompromising refusal to comply with her husband renders her powerless and ineffective and ultimately sweeps her from the scene. The positive antipode to her is Esther, who, because she maintains relations (in both the sexual and the general sense) with Ahasuerus, is able to gain power and to achieve goals higher than the maintenance of her own dignity—the goals of the survival of

---

[74]For a speculation as to Vashti's motivation for refusing to appear, see Elias Bickerman, *Four Strange Books of the Bible,* New York, 1967, 185–86. On the basis of Greek evidence, he argues that "[b]y coming to the king's party, Vashti would lose face, she would degrade herself to the position of a concubine" (185).

[75]Herodotus 1:8–12; Plato, *Republic,* 2:359–360.

her people and of herself. The Jewish and Christian traditions have shared this negative reading of Vashti. Talmudic tradition tends to see her as the grand-daughter of the wicked Nebuchadnezzar; one rabbi teaches that she was summoned "[o]n the seventh day" (Esth. 1:10) because she used to strip Jewish women naked and make them work on the Sabbath. Needless to say, the rabbis saw Ahasuerus as equally lewd and inhumane.[76] In Christian allegory, Vashti was sometimes seen as the Synagogue, that is, as the disobedient woman justly replaced by the faithful wife, the Church (=Esther).[77]

3. The Cabinet Meets
in Emergency Session (1:13–22)

1:13 Then the king consulted with the sages learned in precedents (for it was the royal practice to confer with all who are trained in law and justice). 14 Those closest to him were Carshena, Shethar, Admatha, Tarshish, Meres, Marsena, and Memucan, the seven ministers of Persia and Media who had access to the king's presence and occupied the first rank in the kingdom. 15 "According to law,[a] [he asked,] what should be done to Queen Vashti for not executing the command of King Ahasuerus, conveyed by the eunuchs?"

1:16 Then Memucan said in the presence of the king and the ministers: "Not against the king alone has Queen Vashti committed an offense, but against all the officials and all the peoples who are in all the provinces of King Ahasuerus. 17 When word of what the queen has done comes to all the women, this will make them regard their husbands with contempt; they will say, 'King Ahasuerus ordered Queen Vashti to be brought before him, but she did not come.' 18 This very day the noble ladies of Persia and Media, who have heard what the queen has done, will tell it[b] to all Your Majesty's officials, and there will be endless contempt and rage. 19 If it please Your Majesty, let a royal edict go forth from You, and let it be inscribed in the laws of Persia and Media, so that it will not be revoked, that Vashti shall not come into King Ahasuerus's presence, and let Your Majesty bestow her queenship upon another woman more worthy than she. 20 When this royal decree that Your Majesty will enact is heard throughout Your empire—vast though it is—all wives shall treat their husbands with honor, from the highest to the lowest." 21 The proposal pleased the king and the ministers, and the king enacted what Memucan had proposed. 22 Letters were sent to all the king's provinces,

[76]E.g., *b. Meg.* 12b.
[77]See Marie-Louise Thérel, "L'origine du thème de la 'synagogue répudiée,'" *Scriptorium* 25 (1971): 288–89.

to each and every province in its own script and to each and every people in its own language, that each man shall be master of his household
and speak the language of his people.[c]

a. It is tempting to place the division of the verse after *kĕdāt*, as the *BHS, inter alia*,
proposes: the seven ministers, then, "occupied the first rank in the kingdom, according
to law (or, royal decree)." Given the official and legalistic tone of the following ex-
changes, however, it is better to leave *kĕdāt* where it is, as the first word of v. 15.

b. "[I]t" has to be supplied *ad sensum*, understanding the quoted material in the previous verse as the antecedent. The anomalous absence of an object for *'āmar* has
sometimes caused an emendation of *tō'marnâ* ("will tell") to *timreynâ/tamreynâ* ("will
revolt"). This, however, introduces another anomaly, since the verb *mrh* takes a direct
object or the preposition *b*, but not *l*, as here.[78]

c. This last phrase (*ûmĕdabbēr kilšôn 'ammô*) is difficult. Its unclarity, its absence
in the LXX, and its resemblance to *wā'ām kilšônô* ("every people in its own language")
a few words earlier have often given rise to a suspicion of dittography. But see the discussion in the commentary.

Since the invitation that Queen Vashti refused was to a state banquet and
was delivered in person by the seven royal eunuchs (1:10–11), the refusal pre-
cipitates a state crisis. Rather than handling the matter through quiet diplomacy
and with a personal touch—Vashti is, after all, his wife and not some upstart
courtier—King Ahasuerus characteristically and somewhat comically summons the "sages learned in precedents" (1:13), in particular another set of
seven, the highest-ranking ministers in the empire (v. 14).[79] Because the term
'ittîm in v. 13, rendered above as "precedents," is the plural of one of the Hebrew words for "time," it has been suggested the expertise in question lies in
the realm of astrology rather than or at least in addition to law, as indicated by
the last clause in the verse. Some scholars have gone so far as to emend *'ittîm*
to *dātîm*, "laws,"[80] though the parallel in 1 Chron. 12:33 argues against such a
move. The distinction between astrology and law should not be overdrawn; the
former can act in the service of the latter.[81] The theme of the fit time and the
appropriate season recurs in 3:7, when Haman casts the *pûr* (that is, the lot) for
each day and each month in order to determine the appropriate time to annihilate the Jewish people. Here, too, there is a whiff of astrology, but it is astrology that fails; for the chosen day proves to be one of triumph for the Jews and
disgraceful defeat for the anti-Semites (9:1). So also in chap. 1, there is more

[78]See Gerleman, 68.

[79]It has been pointed out that if one reads the names of the seven royal eunuchs in v. 10 in reverse order, they show some remarkable similarities to this list of seven royal ministers in v. 14.
See Duchesne-Guillemin, "Les noms."

[80]E.g., Moore, *Esther*, 9.

[81]See Bardtke, 287.

than a hint of an expertise that is out of touch with the realities of life and will only worsen the human situation to which it is applied.

The question that Ahasuerus poses to his councillors in 1:15 is redolent of legalism and altogether lacking in feeling. The issue is one of precedent and procedure; the element of human relations fails to come into the king's view. Once again, the office is paramount; the man who holds it uses it to hide from personal responsibility. The council of ministers that is called to deliberate the king's inability to make his wife come to his party is a masterpiece of satire. Memucan's counsel in vv. 16–18 only adds to the reader's sense that unreality dominates in the highest councils of state and that matters are spiraling out of control. His view that Queen Vashti has committed an offense not only against the king but against all the officials and even all the peoples in the empire exhibits an extreme lack of proportion. The offense (if such it really was) is being vastly inflated, but in the absence of Vashti or anything upon which to rely other than legal and astrological precedent, no reality check will be possible. In this aspect, the scene is a preview of Haman's catastrophic lack of a sense of reality as he hatches his genocidal plot. Haman, too, is unable to size up the actual situation, though those close to him can (6:13), and he, too, is missing all sense of proportion. The analogy is close: Memucan's belief that if word gets out about what Vashti has done, *all* the ladies in the empire will imitate her, presages Haman's refusal "to lay hands on Mordecai alone": Instead, *all* the Jews throughout the empire must be destroyed (3:6).

In Memucan's anxiety about an uprising by the female population, the irony is exquisite, for at the end of the next chapter (2:21–23), an insurrection will indeed be in the works—not against all the noblemen of the empire, but only against Ahasuerus, and it will be detected not by the king's "sages learned in precedents" and "trained in law and justice" or by his highest ministers (1:13–14), but by the Jewish exile Mordecai. Whereas they nervously fantasize about impending revolution, blowing the matter out of all proportion and urging the promulgation of formal imperial edicts, he, with his ear to the ground, quietly acts to squelch a genuine conspiracy then unobtrusively goes his way. Not surprisingly, at the end of the tale he, and not they, stands closest to the king (10:3).

The edict itself is also not without irony. As Clines remarks, "the royal decree to all the provinces announcing Vashti's dismissal will give more publicity to Vashti's deed—and her cause—as well as to the king's embarrassment than could ever have been achieved by the mere rumour his courtiers had feared (1:17)."[82] Note also the irony for refusing to come into the king's presence: Vashti (she is no longer "Queen Vashti") shall not come into his presence again (1:19). Unless we are to understand that the sentence entails death

---

[82]Clines, 33.

or imprisonment as well, we may rightfully suspect that Vashti greeted the edict with something other than grief. "[L]et Your Majesty bestow her queenship upon another woman more worthy than she" (*yittēn hammelek lir'ûtāh haṭṭôbâ mimmennâ*) is strikingly reminiscent of 1 Sam. 15:28, Samuel's remark to Saul that "the LORD has this day torn the kingship over Israel from you and has given it to another who is worthier than you" (*ûnĕtānāh lĕrē'ăkā haṭṭôb mimmekkā*). This sets up an analogy between Vashti and Saul, the two monarchs deposed in favor of successors enveloped by a mysterious grace, David and Esther. The reminiscence of Saul might seem coincidental were it not for a number of other associations with him in the book of Esther (see the commentary on 2:5 and 3:1).

The notion that the laws of Persia and Media cannot be revoked (1:19) recurs in 8:8 and also appears in Dan. 6:9, 13. There is, alas, no extrabiblical evidence for it, and Fox is surely right that "it seems an impossible rule for running an empire."[83] The notion does, nonetheless, add to the dramatic intensity of the narrative. Since he cannot repeal his original order to assault the Jews, Ahasuerus must issue a counter-edict that permits the Jews to defend themselves on the same day (as if an edict were necessary for this!) (8:11–12).

Memucan's expectation of the results of the proposed edict (1:20) parallels his fears of what will happen without it. Instead of the women "regard[ing] their husbands with contempt" (v. 17), they will "treat their husbands with honor"; similarly, "from the highest to the lowest" corresponds to "all the officials and all the peoples," against whom Memucan thinks poor Vashti has committed grievous offense (v. 16). Verse 22 is a satirical gem— the report of an imperial edict that "each man shall be master of his household," issued by a monarch who has proven unable to master his own wife. "[A]nd speak the language of his own people" is a problematic expression, often interpreted or emended to refer to the "letters." The documents themselves, that is, are to come to each man in his native language.[84] In that case, the end of the verse refers not to the content of the edict, but to the multilingual character of its issuance. Against this, one can cite Neh. 13:23–24, which complains of children of mixed blood who speak the language of their Gentile mothers rather than the Hebrew of their Jewish fathers. If this oft-cited text is relevant to Esth. 1:22, one point of the decree is to establish the father as the ruling figure in the household. That the goal should have been attempted through an imperial edict is a comic touch that testifies to Ahasuerus's nearly fatal tendency to confuse the personal and the political, to utilize the vast powers of his office to compensate for his deficiencies of character. Here again a strong analogy with Haman is suggested, for Haman, too, seeks a political so-

---

[83]Fox, *Character*, 22.
[84]E.g., Gerleman, 70.

lution to his personal problem posed by an individual who will not do him homage (3:12–14). The Talmudic authority Rava astutely commented that were it not for these first letters decreeing what for him was obvious—that every man should rule in his own household—the populace would not have waited until the appointed day to carry out the genocidal orders in the second set of letters, those instigated by Haman.[85] The absurdity of Memucan's proposal ultimately undermined Haman's, though both carried the day with the malleable emperor. The author's satire of the Persian administrative structure and style thus dominates the account of the deliberations in 1:13–22 and gives some subtle but essential previews of the major action of the book.

4. The Search for Miss Persia and Media Commences (2:1–4)

2:1 Some time later, when King Ahasuerus's rage had abated, he remembered Vashti and what she had done and what had been decreed against her. 2 The king's servants who attended him personally said, "Let beautiful young virgins be sought out for Your Majesty; 3 let Your Majesty appoint commissioners in all the provinces of Your empire to gather every beautiful young virgin into the fortified compound of Susa, to the harem quarters under the administration of Hegai,[a] the king's eunuch in charge of the women. Let them be provided with cosmetics, 4 and let the maiden who pleases Your Majesty be queen in place of Vashti. The advice pleased the king, and he acted upon it.

a. The MT reads here *hēge'*, but the person is clearly the same as the *hēgay* mentioned in vv. 8 and 15.

Chapter 2:1 reminds us that King Ahasuerus's rage, brought on by Queen Vashti's refusal to come to his banquet (1:12), had not abated during the ridiculous cabinet meeting of 1:16–21. The king's decision to issue the edict that "each man shall be master of his household and speak the language of his people" (1:22) was therefore issued when he was still incensed. According to the moral advice of the biblical sages, this is not a good sign. "Better to be forbearing [or, slow to anger] than mighty," Prov. 16:32 warns, / "to have self-control than to conquer a city." This is clearly not a monarch possessed of the self-control necessary to make wise decisions. His rage is one of his outstanding characteristics; it will reappear when Esther identifies his prime minister as the architect of the anti-Jewish plot (7:7), and it does not finally abate until Haman is impaled (7:10). The word for "rage" (*ḥēmâ*) can also have

85*b. Meg.* 12b.

associations with wine (as in Hos. 7:5), and there may be an implication that intoxication as well as anger has played a role in bringing him to his present straits.[86]

How long Ahasuerus was perturbed is hard to determine. Esther is not taken to his palace until four years after Vashti's removal (2:16; 1:3). There may be a hint of comedy in the length of his period of anger and in the king's remembering the cause of his rage only after he calms down (2:1). In the Hebrew Bible, the verb "to remember" (*zākar*), however, often carries with it a note of compassion (as in Gen. 40:14; Lev. 26:42, 45; Jer. 2:2): one "remembers" someone to the latter's advantage. The implication of 2:1 is that Ahasuerus has become melancholy in the absence of his wife and regretful of the severity of her punishment. Fox points out that "[t]he passive verb ["what had been decreed against her"] reminds us that this was not his independent decision" and that he is here subtly "transferring blame to his advisers—a habit he will manifest again."[87] Another example is 7:5–7, when Ahasuerus flies into a paroxysm of rage at hearing of an anti-Jewish plot that he, in fact, had personally approved (3:10–14).

Once again, it is the king's servants (in this case, the royal valets) who suggest a way forward (2:2). Their recommendation that "beautiful young virgins be sought out" for the king is perhaps based on a notion that like the high priest, the king may marry only a virgin (Lev. 21:13).[88] The closest narrative analogy is the procurement of the beautiful young virgin Abishag the Shunammite for King David as he suffered in his old age from hypothermia and perhaps similar problems as well (1 Kings 1:1–4). In the Talmud, an interesting difference is noted: David's courtiers did not propose the appointment of commissioners to gather in the virgins (cf. Esth. 2:3). The rabbi who points this out thinks that whereas the fathers in David's situation willingly brought their daughters, those in Ahasuerus's day sought to hide their daughters from the lecherous monarch.[89] This is probably an overreading. The more likely reason for the difference is that *everything* in Ahasuerus's realm is absurdly bureaucratized; even the king's sex life requires commissioners. The personal has become the political, and both have become laughable. Hakham notes that Esth. 2:3 bears significant points of affinity also to Gen. 41:34–35, in which Joseph proposes that Pharaoh appoint commissioners to gather grain into the store cities during the coming seven years of plenty.[90] If the similarity is deliberate, there may be a disparagement of the king and his court implied in the analogy of women to grain. Connections, verbal and other, with

---

[86]Hakham, 12.
[87]Fox, *Character*, 26.
[88]Paton, 164.
[89]*b. Meg.* 12b.
[90]Hakham, 13.

the story of Joseph in Genesis 37–50 are abundant in Esther,[91] as we shall see repeatedly.

The advice of the king's personal attendants in Esth. 2:2–4 has points in common with Memucan's proposal in 1:16–20 and with chap. 1 in general.[92] "[B]e queen in place of Vashti" (2:4) recalls "bestow her queenship upon another woman more worthy than she" (1:19). In both cases, the proposal/advice "pleased the king," though what the king said to indicate this is tellingly omitted (1:21; 2:4). One has the sense that ideas "please the king" the same way the chosen virgin will "please" him—that is, in a gross, physical way. One may note as well that Memucan spoke of *all* wives just as the king's attendants speak of *all* virgins (1:17; 2:3). Moderation and gradualism are not the strong suits of this court.

What precisely is meant by the expression "be queen" (*timlōk*) is ambiguous. It may mean simply that the maiden will become the consort of the king, but it may also signify, in Zefira Gitay's words, "her taking an active role in ruling the land of Ahasuerus." Eventually, as Gitay notes, Esther "manages to establish herself as an authoritative queen not only by her beauty, but also by her personality and her wisdom."[93] The empire-wide search for a new queen and the selection of a Jewess lack external corroboration and seem improbable. What 2:1–4 may lack if taken for a factual report, it gains if seen as narrative artistry.

5. A Jewish Exile and His Comely Cousin (2:5–7)

2:5 Now there was in the fortified compound of Susa a Jew by the name of Mordecai, son of Jair, son of Shimei, son of Kish, a Benjaminite, **6** who had been exiled from Jerusalem with the group that was carried into exile along with Jeconiah, king of Judah, whom Nebuchadnezzar, king of Babylon, had driven into exile. **7** He was the foster father to Hadassah (that is, Esther), his uncle's daughter, for she had neither father nor mother. The maiden was highly attractive, and when her father and mother had died, Mordecai took her in as a daughter.

The word order alone shows that a new scene is upon us (*'îš yĕhûdî hāyâ*, lit. "A Jewish man there was . . ."; cf. Job 1:1). The contrast between the

---

[91]See Berg, *The Book,* 123–42; Moshe Gan, "The Book of Esther in the Light of the Story of Joseph in Egypt" (Hebrew), *Tarbiz* 31 (1961–62): 144–49; Ludwig A. Rosenthal, "Die Josephsgeschichte mit den Büchen Ester und Daniel verglichen," *ZAW* 15 (1895): 278–84.

[92]Hakham, 13.

[93]Zefira Gitay, "Esther and the Queen's Throne," in *A Feminist Companion to Esther, Judith and Susanna,* ed. Athalya Brenner, FCB 7, Sheffield, 1991, 140–41.

situation of Mordecai and Esther and that of Ahasuerus and Vashti could not be bolder. While the Persians are aristocrats living amid legendary opulence, exercising power worldwide, and partying with abandon, the Jews are kingless and in exile, where they have been driven by a foreign conqueror. In fact, v. 6 employs the root of the word for exile (*glh*) in four distinct constructions, lest the full measure of the Jewish plight be overlooked. The particular mirrors the general: Hadassah's plight resembles that of her people. As they have lost their king and their land and taken up residence in a foreign country, so has she lost her father and her mother, become adopted by her cousin, and taken a foreign name (v. 7).

Why Mordecai was within the royal complex (v. 5) is unclear. Since we find him within the palace gate (2:19) and among the royal courtiers (3:2), it is reasonable to suppose that he holds some office even at the start of the story in the MT as in chap. A. Whether he has let his Jewishness be known is also unclear. According to 2:10 and 20, Mordecai had forbidden Esther to reveal her ethnicity, and 3:4 may imply that he disclosed his origins only in response to questions about why he would not bow to Haman. In this regard, it is interesting that unlike his young cousin, Mordecai has only a Gentile name, one derived, in fact, from the name of the Babylonian god Marduk. Even though he is throughout the story very much "Mordecai the Jew" (6:10), he is acutely aware of the precariousness of his people's position in exile and the need for circumspection in dealing with the host culture. This makes his persistent refusal to bow down to Haman (whatever its rationale) all the more courageous.

Mordecai's genealogy (2:5) is highly reminiscent of the introduction of Saul in 1 Sam. 9:1, more so than coincidence allows. Saul's father and Mordecai's great-grandfather bear the identical name, Kish; both heroes are from the tribe of Benjamin. Shimei is the name not only of Mordecai's grandfather, but also of a member of Saul's clan who curses David for supposedly usurping their throne (2 Sam. 16:5–8). Ibn Ezra, a Jewish commentator of the twelfth century, counters these associations of Mordecai with Saul, of which the midrash makes so much, by arguing that if the text wants us to see Mordecai as descended from Saul, surely it would mention the ancient king himself, as Mordecai's most distinguished ancestor.[94] This objection has some weight. Even on biblical chronology, Mordecai would have to be more than two generations later than Saul, who in fact lived more than half a millennium before Xerxes. We should not assume that Mordecai is a *descendant* of Saul, only that the two are to be thought of together. The relationship is principally contrastive. Whereas Saul lost his throne for sparing Agag, the king of the Amalekites, the archetypical enemy of the Israelites and their God (1 Samuel

---

[94]Ibn Ezra to 2:5.

15), Mordecai gains the premiership by defeating Haman the Agagite (3:1). It is not that the narrator has simply reused two traditional Benjaminite names, Kish and Shimei, nor that he wishes us to think Saul was Mordecai's ancestor. Rather, he uses names from the story of Saul to highlight the significance of Mordecai and Esther's deeds within the larger history of redemption. Mordecai rises on the very point on which Saul fell. His becoming prime minister of the Persian empire (10:2) recaptures some of the glory of monarchy that Saul lost for sparing the first Agagite and that the house of David, Saul's successor "worthier than [he]" (1 Sam. 15:28), finally lost ten years after Jeconiah went into exile.

In the Hebrew Bible, the term *yĕhûdî*, "Jew," applied to Mordecai in 2:5 (and often in Esther), usually denotes a member of the tribe of Judah. In the Talmud there appear several engaging midrashim purporting to explain how Mordecai could have been both a Judahite and a Benjaminite. For example, it is said that he had one parent from each tribe, or that the term "Judahite" refers to one who repudiates idolatry, regardless of ethnicity.[95] At the level of plain sense, however, these harmonistic and homiletical explanations fail. What has actually happened is that in the wake of the exile of the only tribal unit still intact, Judah, the ethnic term *yĕhûdî* came to refer to *any* Israelite; hence our translation "Jew" rather than "Judahite." Mordecai is a Jew because he comes from Judah, the last commonwealth of the people of Israel before the exile, and lives in the community of Jewish/Judahite exiles in Susa. He is a Benjaminite because Benjamin is his ancestral tribal affiliation. In this more general meaning, *yĕhûdî* is a postexilic innovation. Ironically, it is not one with a large resonance in the ongoing Jewish tradition. Though the term "Jew" need not be derogatory and is regularly applied by Jews to themselves, it has never supplanted the older, more scriptural term "Israelite." For good reason, the Jewish people, like the modern Jewish state, is not called "Judah" or "Judea," but "Israel."

The exile of Jeconiah, king of Judah, to which 2:6 refers, occurred in 597 B.C.E. (see 2 Kings 24:8–17). If the verse means that Mordecai was among those taken into exile with him, then there may be an implication that he was one of "the notables of the land" (2 Kings 24:15), as befits a person related to an ancient king. But if so, Mordecai must have been at least 114 when the action of the Masoretic Esther begins in 483 B.C.E., Xerxes's third regnal year (Esth. 1:3)—a most unlikely prospect. Traditionally, some have attempted to circumvent this problem by identifying the antecedent of "whom" in 2:6 as Kish, in the previous verse: it was Mordecai's great-grandfather who was driven into exile from Jerusalem in 597 B.C.E. This is possible, but it depends upon the assumption that the book of Esther must constitute an accurate report

[95]*b. Meg.* 12b–13a.

of historical data, an assumption that we have already had repeated occasion to doubt (cf. A:3). It is more likely that the mention of Jeconiah and the exile is intended to give this late book a "biblical" connection and to set its narrative into the larger framework of the history of redemption of the people Israel. The same can be said for the subtle and indirect evocation of Saul and Agag.

It is not known what rules or expectations governed Mordecai's adoption of his orphaned cousin (2:7), for neither the Hebrew Bible nor even the massive legal canon of rabbinic Judaism provides for adoption (though the rabbis do warmly commend one who raises another's child). The Greek version and rabbinic midrashim tend to see the relationship between Mordecai and Hadassah (Esther) as one of marriage,[96] and ancient custom does indeed know of adoption in anticipation of matrimony (cf. Ezek. 16:1–14). It is more likely, however, that these Jewish readings are motivated by a desire to avoid the thought that Ahasuerus and Esther, a Gentile and a Jew, were indeed married, since Jewish law does not grant legitimacy to an interreligious union. Whatever the precise nature of Mordecai's adoption of Hadassah, the act stands in patent contrast to Ahasuerus's summoning of the virgins in 2:1–4. Where Ahasuerus takes the maidens away from their families, Mordecai assumes the role of father to a maiden who has lost her parents. Where Ahasuerus acts with royal power and in a bureaucratic manner to satisfy his lust, Mordecai acts privately and within traditional family structures to provide for someone else. By the end of the tale, Mordecai's quiet loyalty and conscientiousness will have saved the lives of both Ahasuerus and the whole Jewish people.

The name "Hadassah" (missing in the Greek versions and in the rest of the Masoretic Esther) seems to mean "myrtle" (cf. Isa. 41:19), and thus fits with a number of Hebrew female names derived from plant names (e.g., "Tamar," the date-palm). The etymology of "Esther" is less certain. It may derive from a Persian word cognate with the English "star" or from the name of the Babylonian goddess Ishtar. There are, appropriately, two good explanations as to why Mordecai's foster daughter has dual names. "Hadassah" may have been the name she used in Jewish circles, and Esther, the one she used in the larger, predominantly Gentile world (cf. Dan. 1:6–7, in which Daniel and his three friends are assigned Babylonian names once they are in exile). Alternatively, Hadassah may have been her personal name, and Esther, the throne-name assigned her upon her coronation but used by the author of the book even earlier (cf. 2 Kings 23:34, in which the Pharaoh Neco changes a Judahite prince's name when he installs him as a puppet king). Of these two possibilities, the former is the more likely.

---

[96]LXX to 2:7 and *b. Meg.* 13a. See n. 54.

6. Esther Wins
the Beauty Contest (2:8–20)

2:8 When the king's order and his edict were proclaimed, and large numbers of maidens were gathered into the fortified compound of Susa under the supervision of Hegai, Esther was taken into the royal palace, into the custody of Hegai, the harem-keeper. 9 The maiden pleased him and attracted his favor, and he made haste to provide her with her cosmetics and her delicacies along with seven picked maidens from the royal palace. He gave her and her maidens an advantage[a] in the harem.

2:10 (Now Esther had not disclosed her people and her family, for Mordecai had forbidden her to do so. 11 Every day Mordecai would walk around in front of the courtyard of the harem in order to find out how Esther was faring and what was happening to her.)

2:12 The prescribed beauty treatment for the women took a full twelve months: six months with oil of myrrh and six months with perfumes and women's cosmetics. At the end, each maiden's turn to go to King Ahasuerus arrived, 13 and whatever she requested would be given to her to take with her from the harem to the king's quarters. 14 In the evening she would go, and in the morning she would come back to a different harem under the custody of Shaashgaz, the king's eunuch in charge of the concubines. She would not go to the king again unless he found pleasure in her and she was summoned by name. 15 When the turn came for Esther, daughter of Abihail, the uncle of Mordecai (who had taken her in as a daughter), to go to the king, she asked for nothing except what Hegai, the king's eunuch in charge of the women, advised. But all who saw her found Esther charming. 16 Esther was taken to King Ahasuerus, in his royal palace, in the tenth month—that is, the month of Tebeth—in the seventh year of his reign. 17 The king preferred Esther over all the other women, and she won his grace and favor more than all the other virgins. So he put a royal diadem on her head and made her queen in place of Vashti. 18 The king then gave a great banquet for all his officials and his courtiers—"the banquet of Esther." He also proclaimed a remission of taxes for the provinces and distributed gifts, as befitted the king's liberality.

2:19 When the virgins were gathered a second time,[b] Mordecai was sitting in the palace gate, 20 but Esther still did not disclose her family and her people, as Mordecai had forbidden her. For Esther continued to do what Mordecai told her, just as when she was his ward.

a. The verb *wayšannehā* in the *qal* means "to do again, repeat." Esther 2:9 is its only appearance in the Bible in the *pi'el* with this meaning. Ehrlich notes a rabbinic usage with the sense of "mark out, distinguish,"[97] which seems to fit best with *lĕṭôb* (lit., "for the good") later in the verse. The latter may be the infinitive ("for being successful"). Hence, our rendering of "gave . . . an advantage."

b. This very problematic first clause is missing in the Greek and suspect in the MT, but sense can be made of it. See the commentary.

Chapter 2:8 resumes the narrative of v. 4 after the interruption that introduced the two Jewish protagonists. Traditional Jewish commentators have been anxious to demonstrate that Mordecai did not willingly send his foster daughter/wife into the bedroom of the lecherous Ahasuerus and that Esther, too, did not oblige of her own free will. But the verb ("was taken") at best demonstrates her passivity; it says nothing about her volition.[98] The favor Esther finds in the eyes of Hegai, the royal harem-keeper (v. 9), foreshadows the favor she will find with Ahasuerus himself (v. 17) and, more distantly, the favor that Mordecai will find among his kinsmen (10:3). It also has a rich resonance outside the book of Esther. Like Esther, Joseph as a slave in Egypt finds favor with his master Potiphar, though there the reason is given: ". . . his master saw that the LORD was with him" (Gen. 39:3). Probably we are to think of the same causation here, except that a lack of editorializing is characteristic of our author's style, just as the omission of direct reference to God is characteristic of his theology. In any event, the parallel between Esther's rise under the custody of Hegai and Joseph's in Potiphar's house is suggestive. An even closer analogy is that of Daniel and his three friends in their enforced royal service to the Babylonian king. When Daniel requested a special diet, "God disposed the chief officer to be kind and compassionate toward Daniel" (Dan. 1:9). Here, too, the results amply vindicate the officer's divinely induced predisposition—and the four youths' religious scruples as well (Dan. 1:8–9, 15). Hegai's assignment to Esther of the seven ladies-in-waiting foreshadows future success similar to that of Joseph and Daniel; it augurs her coming queenship (cf. the king's seven eunuchs in Esth. 1:10).

The term "delicacies" (*mānôt*) in Esth. 2:9 foreshadows the use of the same term in 9:19 and 22, where it refers to the presents of food that Jews send to each other as part of the celebration of Purim. In the Hebrew Bible, food presents a problem for Jews in foreign courts, just as it does today for Jews who observe *kashrut* (the dietary laws) outside the home, as Jewish law requires. This is, as we have seen, a major issue in Daniel 1; the same point appears pointedly in Judith 12:2 (see also Tobit 1:10). It should not, however, be read

[97]Arnold B. Ehrlich, *Randglossen zur Hebräischen Bibel,* Leipzig, 1914, 7:112 (hereafter this volume will be identified as "Ehrlich").
[98]Contra Hakham, 15.

into Esth. 2:9.[99] *Kashrut* in whatever stage of its development is nowhere to be found in Esther, neither when she is disguising her Jewishness nor afterward. The realm of religious observance seems quite distant from the circles that produced the book of Esther.

Chapter 2:10 introduces a note that is reiterated in 2:20: obeying Mordecai's instructions, Esther concealed her Jewishness. Though both 2:10–11 and 2:20 have an explanatory and parenthetical air to them and may be secondary, their placement is nonetheless significant. The two statements of Esther's compliance with Mordecai's directives bracket the elaborate account of the beauty contest and Esther's selection as its winner (2:12–18). Indeed, the phrases "her people and her family" (v. 10) and "her family and her people" (v. 20) make a nice chiasm[100] and thus suggest the possibility of a deliberate bracketing. The larger point is clear: neither before nor after her elevation to the queenship did Esther break faith with her foster father. She thus assumes the role of the Jew who initially passes for a Gentile in the foreign court and eventually uses his or her high status to rescue his or her endangered people. This role is another point of contact with the story of Joseph (cf. Gen. 41:39–45; 42:7). It is also one shared by Moses (cf. Exod. 2:11–22, esp. v. 19), whose story has a number of suggestive commonalities with Esther's.[101]

There are, however, serious practical problems with this notion that Esther successfully concealed her Jewishness and her connection to Mordecai. Were their consanguinity and his adoption of her unknown? Was no one curious as to where and by whom the new queen had been raised? Did Mordecai's daily trip to the courtyard of the harem (v. 11) not arouse suspicion, and was he not known as a Jew (3:4)? However lacking in verisimilitude it may be, Esther's hiding her Jewishness and her connection to Mordecai is a narrative necessity. Without it, Haman's genocidal plot could never have been launched. With it, her foiling of the plot becomes vastly more powerful, for it coincides with the disclosure of her Jewishness (7:4), so that as in the cases of Joseph and Moses, the national and the personal stories intersect and reinforce each other.

The twelve-month beauty treatment (2:12) is another exaggeration, akin to the hundred-eighty-day party of 1:3–4, 6–8. Perhaps we are to hear a note of contempt for the luxury of the foreign court[102] and its narcissistic and grossly self-indulgent body culture. That "whatever [Esther] requested would be given [*yinnātēn*] to her" (2:13) foreshadows Ahasuerus's words at the two later royal banquets, "What is your wish? It shall be granted [*yinnātēn*] you! What is your request? Up to half the empire—it shall be fulfilled!" (5:6; cf. 7:2 and 9:12).

[99]Contra Paton, 174.
[100]Moore, *Esther,* 22.
[101]See Gerleman, 11–23, 80.
[102]Ibid., 81.

This woman exerts a mysterious charm; things tend to go her way. Similarly, 2:14 introduces a note that will prove crucial to Esther's moment of decision and define her act of greatest courage: "[s]he would not go to the king again unless he found pleasure in her and she was summoned by name" (cf. 4:11, 16). Throughout these first two chapters, terms are being rather innocently introduced that will nevertheless prove essential to the main action of the story: banquet, edict, rebellion, honor, familial loyalty, people, delicacies, summoning. Esther's reluctance to ask for any cosmetics other than what Hegai advises (2:15) may be another suggestive touch, for in the first of those two fateful banquets, she declines Ahasuerus's generous offer "[u]p to half the empire" and asks only for another banquet with him and Haman (5:7–8). Though scholars have long speculated about why she asked for nothing more in 2:15,[103] there is a simple but compelling answer: Having mysteriously won the favor of Hegai (2:9), she wisely relies on his expertise instead of her own instincts. This too may foreshadow her deference to another older man, Mordecai, in her moment of decision (4:16). Both texts imply that she was wise and forbearing rather than impulsive, prideful, and self-destructively independent.

The words "royal palace" in 2:16 connect Esther's triumph with Vashti's disgrace, for it was "in the royal palace of King Ahasuerus" that the latter gave her own party (1:9). Perhaps the second term refers to the queen's quarters[104] and should be revocalized *bêt mĕlākôt* "house of queens."[105] The month of her transfer there, Tebeth, occurs around January. The royal diadem Ahasuerus sets upon her (2:17) recalls his fateful command that Vashti appear before him wearing the same article of attire (1:11). The implication is that at long last he has found the docile sex object that he wants and that Vashti proved not to be — an implication that will be hugely falsified when Esther enters his throne room unsummoned as part of a master plan to counter his own genocidal edict against her people (5:1). Note also what is missing in 2:17 — any mention that Ahasuerus *married* Esther. The queen is, of course, the king's wife, but the author may have avoided marital terminology in order to play down the violation of Jewish law involved in Esther's matrimony with a non-Jew (contrast 1:17, about Vashti, and F:3, which speaks of both a marriage and an elevation to queenship). The "banquet of Esther" in 2:18 reintroduces the theme of banqueting prominent in chap. 1 and once again foreshadows the climactic royal banquets of chaps. 5 and 7 and the Jews' own feasting, first as their day of triumph looms (8:17) and then afterward in the first and every subsequent Purim (9:16–19, 20–23). Similarly, the king's distribution of gifts in 2:18 foreshadows the exchange of gifts that will be a central feature of the observance of the Jew-

---

[103]See Paton, 182.
[104]Hakham, 18.
[105]See Ehrlich, 110.

ish feast (9:22). The "remission" (*hănāḥâ*) that he proclaims in 2:18 probably involved a temporary suspension of taxes. Comparative evidence suggests that it may also have involved relief from military service, the release of prisoners, the distribution of gifts mentioned in the same verse, and the proclamation of a general holiday (cf. Leviticus 25; 1 Macc. 10:25–35).[106] Fox is correct that "[t]he author is hinting that when things go well with the Jews, others benefit too."[107] The empire-wide celebration of "the banquet of Esther" foreshadows the particular Jewish festival of banqueting that will be Purim. It should be noted, however, that though the populace benefited through the remission of taxes and the like, the state treasuries did not ultimately lose because of the advancement of the Jews: After Ahasuerus's promotion of Mordecai the Jew, "King Ahasuerus [successfully] imposed tribute on the mainland and on the islands" (10:1).

"When the virgins were gathered a second time" (2:19) does not appear in the Greek versions. Considering the difficulties posed by this second gathering and the repetition here of the substance of 2:8–10 and 2:19–20, we may be dealing with an instance of textual garbling. Those committed to making sense of the MT have, however, proposed several plausible interpretations: for example, (1) that even after his selection of Esther, Ahasuerus wanted more wives or concubines; (2) that the second gathering of virgins come for "the banquet of Esther" (2:18; cf. Cant. 3:11); (3) that they came in hopes of being chosen as ladies-in-waiting (cf. Ps. 45:13–16); (4) that those maidens coming from far off were still arriving; (5) that 2:19 refers parenthetically to a period earlier than Esther's marriage, or (6) that the verse alludes to a second harem quarter and thus refers to the transference of the virgins from Hegai's area to Shaashgaz's.[108]

II. Mordecai and Esther Save the King's Life

Esther 2:21–23

2:21 In those days, when Mordecai was sitting in the palace gate, Bigthan and Teresh, two of the king's eunuchs who guarded the threshold, became angry and sought to lay hands upon King Ahasuerus. **22** The matter became known to Mordecai, who disclosed it to Queen Esther, and

---

[106]See Moshe Weinfeld, *Justice and Righteousness in Israel and the Nations* (Hebrew), Jerusalem, 1985.

[107]Fox, *Character,* 38.

[108]See Hakham, 19; Paton, 186–87; Fox, *Character,* 38.

Esther told it to the king in Mordecai's name. 23 The matter was investigated and found to be so. The two of them were hanged upon a tree, and all this was recorded in the book of annals in the presence of the king.

This story of Mordecai's foiling the assassination plot of the two eunuchs is rich in suggestive resonances both within the book of Esther and outside it. Fox points out that on the basis of text-critical considerations "[t]his incident [was] probably added by the author of MT-Esther [and notes that it] establishes Mordecai's loyalty before it can be called into question by his violation of the royal decree in 3:3."[109] A courtier who takes action to save the king's life cannot be fairly accused of contempt for the king's laws, as Mordecai and his fellow Jews will be in 3:8. It should also be noted that the insertion of 2:21 here places Mordecai's heroism and Haman's promotion (3:1) back to back, thus setting the stage for a conflict over the question of who is the king's closest and truest friend. The question will be almost completely answered in chap. 6, when it just so happens that the sleepless king, hearing his book of annals read one night, is reminded of Mordecai's outstanding act of service (v. 2) and orders Haman to run through the streets as the herald in the parade to honor his great rival (v. 10).

Mordecai's unobtrusive reporting of the assassination plot through the agency of Esther also foreshadows the more momentous story of their jointly foiling an infinitely larger assassination plot—Haman's attempted genocide of the Jewish people. In that case, the discussions between Mordecai and Esther will have to be carried on by an intermediary, her attendant, the royal eunuch Hatach (chap. 4)—presumably so as to keep Esther's relation to Mordecai and her Jewishness secret. Here, by contrast, she reports the plot "to the king in Mordecai's name" (2:22), which surely should have given away the very information that her foster father had enjoined her not to divulge (2:10, 20). Fox may be right that unless we are to suppose the employment of a mediator here, too, "[t]his might be a slight slip in narrative logic."[110] A better alternative might be to see this as yet another comic touch: This king and this royal court, so paranoid and so bureaucratized in many areas but so lax and neglectful in others, are unable to put two and two together. They fail to associate Esther and Mordecai even when the evidence is glaring, just as they fail to honor the man who reported the assassination plot (6:2–3), and just as the king, at long last cognizant of Mordecai's fidelity and of Haman's wickedness, is incapable of condemning the malefactor until one of his eunuchs instructs him to do so (7:9). Beneath the comic touch lies a serious message: that things work out for the Jews because of the virtue and craftiness of their leaders combined with a mysteriously beneficial set of apparent coincidences (e.g., Mordecai's over-

---

[109]Fox, *Character*, 40. See also Clines, 105.
[110]Fox *Character*, 40.

hearing the plot and the king's hearing the report of it in the book of annals), and not because of any wisdom or goodwill toward Jews on the part of the Persian regime.

A Talmudic authority—R. Hiyya b. Abba, in the name of Rabbi Yochanan—pointed to an important resonance with Esth. 2:21–23 of a story from outside the book of Esther, once again the story of Joseph: "The Holy One, blessed be He, made a master angry at his servants in order to accomplish the will of a righteous man. And who was he? Joseph. . . . [and he made] servants [angry] at their master in order to accomplish a miracle for a righteous man. And who was he? Mordecai. . . . "[111] The immediate connection is the verb *qṣp*, "to become angry," used of Pharaoh with reference to his cupbearer and baker (Gen. 40:2) and of Bigthan and Teresh with reference to King Ahasuerus (Esth. 2:21). Were it not for Pharaoh's angry imprisonment of his cupbearer, Joseph would never have realized his wish to be free (and perhaps to lord it over his brothers as well) (Gen. 41:9–44). And were it not for Bigthan and Teresh's anger at Ahasuerus, Mordecai would never have been honored by the king at Haman's expense (Esther 6). It is worthy of note that in each case there are two royal courtiers who offend the king, and in each case the offense seems to be attempted insurrection. This is clear for Bigthan and Teresh, and the verb *ḥṭ'*, "to sin," in Gen. 40:1 suggests the same offense. It is, in any event, a capital crime, punishable by decapitation and impalement (Gen. 40:19, 22). This latter is precisely the punishment meted out to Bigthan and Teresh (Esth. 2:23). One may further note that as in the case of Joseph, so in that of Mordecai, the exile's good deed goes unnoticed and unregarded until one night their respective kings find themselves unable to sleep (Gen. 41:1–8; Esth. 6:1). More than coincidence allows, these commonalities further argue for the influence of the story of Joseph upon the book of Esther.

The little story of Bigthan and Teresh exhibits one of the major themes of the larger story of the book of Esther, the theme of "measure for measure." Just as Haman is hoist with his own petard, impaled, that is, on the very stake he has set up for Mordecai (7:10), so that the day he has picked for the annihilation of the Jews becomes the day of Jewish triumph over the anti-Semites (9:1), so are Bigthan and Teresh "investigated" (*bqš*, 2:23) for having "sought" (*bqš*, 2:21) to do in the king, and, like Haman, they are impaled for having plotted murder. In both the smaller and the larger story, Mordecai and Esther (the latter acting at the former's behest) are the heroes. Once again, the subtext is that there is no conflict, only a convergence between service to the king and service to the Jewish community. The deliverance of Ahasuerus from his would-be assassins and the deliverance of the Jews from their archenemy Haman are of a piece.

[111]*b. Meg.* 13b.

III. Genocide Decreed against the Jews

Esther 3:1–15

1. Mordecai's Refusal (3:1–6)

3:1 Some time later, King Ahasuerus promoted Haman son of Hamme-datha the Agagite, elevating him and setting his throne above those of all the officials who were with him. **2** All the king's courtiers who were in the king's gate would kneel and bow down to Haman, for such was the king's command concerning him. But Mordecai would not kneel and he would not bow down. **3** Then the king's courtiers who were in the king's gate said to Mordecai, "Why are you violating the king's command?" **4** When they had spoken to him day after day and he did not heed them, they informed Haman in order to see whether Mordecai's explanation would be tolerated, for he had disclosed to them that he was a Jew. **5** When Haman saw that Mordecai was not kneeling or bowing down to him, he was filled with rage. **6** But he considered it beneath his dignity to lay hands on Mordecai alone. Since they had told him who Mordecai's people were, Haman sought to destroy all the Jews in Ahasuerus's empire—the people of Mordecai.[a]

a. The second *'am mordĕkay* ("the people of Mordecai") is missing in the LXX and is quite possibly a dittography from earlier in the same verse. Some scholars emend to *'im*—"with Mordecai."[112] But see the commentary.

In this passage, we are introduced both to Haman, the villain of the book, and to Mordecai's challenge to Haman, which serves as the next complication in this fast-paced narrative. It is possible that the term rendered as "Agagite" in v. 1 is a Persian name of some sort, but given the connections of Mordecai with Saul (see the commentary on 2:5), it is likely that the term is intended to recall the Amalekite king whom Saul spared (1 Samuel 15).[113] The typological significance of the incident of the encounter of Saul and Agag is seen not only in Esther, a much later book than Samuel, but also in an ancient poetic oracle ascribed to Balaam son of Beor and predicting the ascent of an Israelite king (presumably, Saul) over Agag (Num. 24:7). The irony, of course, is that Agag inadvertently served as the agent of Saul's dethronement (1 Sam.

[112]E.g, Moore, *Esther,* 37.
[113]Ibid., 35.

15:13–31). Perhaps the author of Esther wishes us to think that the events set down in this book were the realization of the ascent of the house of Saul and the elevation of Israel prophetically announced already in Num. 24:7.

No reason for Ahasuerus's promotion of Haman in v. 1 is given. Whatever it was, "[t]his verse sets up a sharp contrast between the unrewarded merit of Mordecai and Haman's unmerited rewards."[114] Mordecai saves the king's life (2:21–23) but receives no recognition (see 6:3). Haman has, so far as we know, done nothing for the king, but receives the premiership nonetheless, along with the honor and recognition of everyone except Mordecai (v. 2). Haman's being granted a lofty "throne" may foreshadow regal aspirations, as in 6:8, when he asks to be clothed in royal garb and to ride upon the king's horse. It surely stands in poignant contrast to the oracle in Num. 24:7 about an Israelite king's "ascending over Agag" and having his kingship elevated.

Why Mordecai refuses to kneel before Haman is unknown. That a Jew may bow down to another man is clear from the Bible itself, where this happens repeatedly (e.g., Gen. 23:7; 27:29; 1 Kings 1:31). Some have speculated that Haman claimed divine honors (as Nebuchadnezzar does in Judith 3:8), and thus Mordecai refused to bow out of the traditional Jewish resistance to idolatry. In support of this, one may cite the usage of the verb *kāraʿ* ("kneel"), which occurs twice in v. 2. Though the word need not imply homage, when it does the recipient is nearly always God. The exception is 2 Kings 1:13, wherein the recipient is the prophet Elisha, the "man of God" to whom a captain pleads for his life (as if to God himself). Similarly, the conjunction of kneeling (*kāraʿ*) and bowing down (*hištaḥăwā*) that we see in Esth. 3:2 is otherwise reserved for homage to God.[115] But if idolatry is the cause of Mordecai's noncompliance, the text is strangely silent about this. In addition, it is difficult to see why the king commands that an underling be treated as a god when he himself is not.

Since v. 4 can be interpreted to mean that Mordecai's Jewishness was the cause of his refusal to kneel and bow to Haman, and since idolatry seems an unlikely factor here, some scholars have seen the issue as one of ethnicity. Agag's nation, the Amalekites, had long been conceived as the archetypical enemy of Mordecai's nation, the Israelites or Jews (e.g., Exod. 17:8–16; Deut. 25:17–19). In light of the savagery of the Amalekite assault upon Israel in the wilderness and the perduring imperative upon Israel to annihilate Amalek, for Mordecai to do homage to Haman would, so the theory goes, have been a gross betrayal of his nation's honor.[116] This theory seems possible, but is without corroboration.

The tradition that survives in Esth. A:17 (but not in the MT) provides another possibility. Perhaps Mordecai refused to honor Haman because he knew

---

[114]Ibid.
[115]Ehrlich, 115.
[116]E.g., Moore, *Esther*, 36–37.

that the latter had somehow been associated with the two eunuchs who had conspired to assassinate the king (see the commentary on A:18). Presumably unable to substantiate his suspicion, Mordecai sought another way to provoke Haman and bring him down, just as he had brought down Gabatha and Tharra. Like the other theories about Mordecai's noncompliance, this is possible, but highly unlikely.

Rather than arguing out the various speculations, it would be more helpful to note the literary symmetry between Mordecai's refusal to bow to Haman and Vashti's refusal to come to Ahasuerus's party (1:10–12). In both cases, a mysterious refusal whose cause can only be guessed occasions a catastrophic rage in the one refused (cf. 1:12 with 3:5), as well as a crisis of state and an absurd imperial decree (cf. 1:13–22 with 3:5–13). In each case, an irascible dignitary magnifies a personal slight (albeit one with political overtones) into an all-consuming political issue. A major part of the genius of the plot of Esther is the way the consequences of these two very similar but independent events come to intersect, with enormously positive results for both the Jews and the empire.

The language with which the king's courtiers are said to have inquired about Mordecai's reason for not bowing to Haman is strikingly close to the language of only one other verse in the Hebrew Bible. This is the verse in which Potiphar's wife is said to have persisted in her attempt to seduce Joseph. "When they had spoken to him day after day, and he did not heed them . . . " (*wayhî bě'omrām 'ēlāyw yôm wāyôm wělō' šāma' 'ǎlêhem*, Esth. 3:4) is so similar to "[W]hen she spoke to Joseph day after day, and he did not heed her" (*wayhî kědabběrāh 'el-yôsēp yôm yôm wělō' šāma' 'ēlêyhā*, Gen. 39:10) that one is tempted to suspect influence rather than coincidence. The overall pattern between the story of Mordecai and Esther and the story of Joseph encourages this suspicion. If it is valid, then an analogy is implied between Mordecai's refusal to accommodate Haman and Joseph's stout refusal to yield to his would-be seductress. Perhaps we should go further and infer that just as Joseph was motivated by a fear of betraying his master and sinning grievously against God (Gen. 39:8–9), so Mordecai is motivated by the desire to maintain his authenticity as a Jew—by refusing to accommodate an Amalekite, to engage in idolatry, or whatever. In any event, in each case the refusal results in a false accusation (Gen. 39:13–19; Esth. 3:8), a catastrophic decree against the innocent (Gen. 39:19–20; Esth. 3:9–14), followed by the rescue of the endangered people of Israel (Gen. 45:5–7; Esth. 8:1–14) and the exaltation into the premiership of the man who had adhered so obstinately and so dangerously to his refusal (Gen. 41:37–46; Esth. 8:15–17).

Haman's rage at being slighted is something he shares with Ahasuerus (Esth. 3:5; 2:1). It is, as we have seen, typical of a biblical fool and symptomatic of impending disaster. The courses of action toward which their rage impels these two men are also quite similar. Just as Ahasuerus's decree against Vashti resulted from a worry that women would "regard their husbands with contempt" (*lĕhabzôt*, 1:17; see also "contempt," [*bizzāyôn*] in 1:17), so does Haman "consider it beneath his dignity (*wayyibez*) to lay hands on Mordecai alone" (3:6). And so, just as Ahasuerus issues a decree not only about Vashti but about *all* women in his empire (1:19–20), so Haman engineers a death sentence not only against Mordecai, but against the Jews of *all* 127 provinces (3:12–14). Ironically, it is Haman's gigantic self-regard and his exaggerated fear of disgrace that puts him on the course that will result in his most ignominious disgrace and, finally, self-destruction (7:1–8:2).

Though some scholars are inclined to drop the phrase "the people of Mordecai" (*'am mordĕkāy*) at the end of 3:6 as a dittography of the identical Hebrew phrase ("Mordecai's people") earlier in the verse, our translation adheres to the MT, which underscores Mordecai's status as the representative Jew, both in his current affliction and in his eventual triumph. Other aspects of the same verse suggest an identification of Mordecai with the interests of the Persian administration as well. Haman's desire "to lay hands (*lišlōaḥ yād*)" on Mordecai's people echoes Bigthan and Teresh's plot "to lay hands (*lišlōaḥ yād*) upon King Ahasuerus." Similarly, Haman "sought (*waybaqqēš*) to destroy all the Jews," just as the two assassins had "sought (*waybaqšû*) to lay hands upon King Ahasuerus" (3:6; 2:21). The implication may be that an attack on the Jews is analogous to an attack upon the person of the king himself. In any case, the similarity in phrasing between Haman's plot and that of the two assassins raises the possibility—distant though it may seem in chap. 3—that Mordecai will somehow foil the new conspiracy just as he did the last one.

2. Haman Hatches His Plot (3:7–11)

3:7 In the first month (that is, the month of Nisan) in King Ahasuerus's twelfth year, *pur* (which means "the lot") was cast in the presence of Haman concerning each day and each month. The lot fell on the thirteenth day[a] of the twelfth month (that is, the month of Adar). 8 Then Haman said to King Ahasuerus, "There is a certain people scattered and unassimilated among all the peoples in all the provinces of Your empire. Their laws are different from those of every other people, and they do not keep the king's laws. It is not in Your Majesty's interest to leave them alone. 9 If it please Your Majesty, let there be drawn up an order to annihilate them, and I will pay ten thousand talents of silver to the officials for deposit in the royal treasury." 10 So the king took his signet ring from his hand and gave it to Haman son of Hammedatha the Agagite, the enemy of the Jews. 11 The king said to Haman, "The money is yours and so are the people, to do with as you see fit."

a. The MT lacks the words "[t]he lot fell on the thirteenth day" and seems seriously apocopated. The restoration of the day itself can be justified on the basis of a number of versions, two of which (the LXX and the OL) read "the fourteenth,"[117] but one of which (the AT) reads "the thirteenth" (4:7), which conforms with the MT of 8:12; 9:1, 17. The reading of the LXX and OL may reflect an old variation within the tradition. Note the way in which even the MT makes the fourteenth, and not only the thirteenth, the day of hostilities (9:17–19).

Since 3:7 interrupts the natural flow from v. 6 to v. 8, some scholars have seen it as an interpolation, perhaps inserted to foreshadow the adaptation of the story of Esther and Mordecai to the holiday of Purim (cf. 9:16–32, esp. v. 24). In its location in the MT (as indicated in the translation above), v. 7 can be understood to reflect Haman's desire to find an auspicious date on which to present his plan for genocide to the king.[118] In the AT, however, the substance of this verse does not precede but rather follows Haman's receiving permission to annihilate the Jews (AT 4:7). Since in the MT Haman does not cast lots again, the AT seems to win the point here: We are to understand that the lots are cast to determine the date of the pogrom, not the date on which to propose it to King Ahasuerus.[119]

Even with the emended translation of 3:7 that appears above, it is odd that we lack the date in Nisan when the lots were cast, which appears in no version. The casting of lots for every month of the year, from the first to the twelfth, reflects an elaborate astrological ritual and suggests the magnitude of Haman's trust in fate. The month in which this takes place, Nisan, recalls, however, an elaborate ritual that is anything but astrological—the ritual of Passover, which also occurs in the first month, or Nisan (Exodus 12). As the story works out, it is the dynamic of *redemption,* represented by Nisan, rather than the dynamic of *fate,* represented by Haman's lots (*pûrîm*), that triumphs (see 9:1).

Haman's introduction to his genocidal proposal (3:8) is a rhetorical masterpiece as subtle in construction as it is malevolent in intent. As Fox points out, "[h]e begins with a truth stated in a way that makes the facts appear sinister, then slides into a half-lie, then into full lies."[120] The truth he states is that the Jews are scattered and unassimilated (or, "separate"; Heb. *mĕpōrād*). Usually the Hebrew Bible views the differentness of the Jews in a positive light. Especially close to Esth. 3:5 is Num. 23:9b, in which a Gentile prophet pays tribute to the specialness of Israel: "See, it is a people who dwells apart and is not reckoned among the nations." Similarly, Deut. 4:5–8 sees in the differentness of Israel's law the source of Gentile admiration for the wisdom of Israel

---

[117]See the table in Fox, *Character,* 278.
[118]E.g., by Paton, 201.
[119]Michael V. Fox, *Redaction,* SBLMS 40, Atlanta, 1991, 80–81.
[120]Fox, *Character,* 47–48.

and their closeness to God. Haman's half-lie is that these laws are altogether different from those of other peoples. His full lies are that the Jews disobey the king's laws and must therefore be annihilated. Haman cleverly neglects to mention the name of this problematic people, though, as Moore observes, by so doing "Haman himself has unwittingly set the stage for Esther's unexpected opposition and her victory over him."[121] Ahasuerus's failure even to ask the name of the offending nation before authorizing its total obliteration does not speak well for him, but it does give him the loophole of claiming that he did not know Haman planned to destroy Queen Esther's people (chap. 7), and this, in turn, enables the Jews to avoid the daunting and probably suicidal prospect of opposing the king himself.

Haman's speech in 3:8–9 has much in common with Memucan's in 1:16–20.[122] In each case, a personal slight—Vashti's to Ahasuerus, Mordecai's to Haman—is magnified out of all proportion and transformed into a state crisis. In each case, the damage to the king from the act of disobedience is the basis for a draconian edict aimed not only at the alleged malefactor, but at the whole class of people to whom she or he belongs. Finally, the advantage to the king of accepting the suggestion is stressed. One difference is that whereas Ahasuerus is a witness to Vashti's insubordination, he must rely on Haman to relay Mordecai's and thus cannot—or at least does not—seek to check his premier's accuracy. Had he done so, he would have learned the crucial datum that Haman slyly omits, though it is obvious to the readers: Mordecai has refused to bow to Haman himself. Though Haman's ego brings about the state crisis— and eventually his downfall—he is clever enough to keep his ego out of his presentation to the king, where it could only impede acceptance of his vindictive plan.

The verb rendered above as "to leave them alone" (*lĕhannîḥām*, 3:8) is another point of irony. It is from the very same root (*nwḥ*) that will be used to report that the Jews "rested" after defeating the anti-Semites (9:17–18) and "obtained relief from their enemies" (9:22). Haman's ego-driven plan to deprive the Jews of rest becomes the source of their higher and more enduring rest. His short-lived, frenetic hatred gives birth to their annual, leisurely merrymaking.

That Haman offers the king a bribe in order to have the Jews exterminated (3:9) lowers our opinion of each of them. The astronomical amount offered— "2/3 of the annual income of the empire" according to one scholar's calculation[123]—shows the degree of Haman's obsession and the magnitude of what he stands to lose if the plan backfires. Ahasuerus, for his part, ought to have

---

[121]Moore, *Esther,* 38.

[122]Paton, 203, and Hakham, 28. Note that a Tannaitic tradition identifies the two men (*b. Meg.* 12b).

[123]Paton, 205. See Herodotus 3:95.

suspected that Haman would not be making so generous an offer of his own
wealth if the issue were only the well-being of the king's authority, as Haman
artfully pretends in 3:8. Ahasuerus's acceptance of the proposal in 3:10 is strikingly reminiscent of Pharaoh's commissioning of Joseph in Gen. 41:42, but the
context is diametrically opposed: Whereas Joseph's elevation works to the
benefit of everyone and saves the lives of the Israelites, Haman's elevation
brings about violence throughout the empire and is intended to end the lives of
its Jewish population. Joseph rises because of his God-given ability to avert
tragedy and promote life (Gen. 41:33–43; 45:5); Haman rises because of his
fiendish hatred and the extent to which he will go to murder his enemies. The
text of Esth. 3:10 communicates the enormity of his malevolence not only by
reference to his Agagite ancestry (see the commentary on 2:5 and 3:1), but also
by the initial use of the fearful epithet "the enemy of the Jews," which will recur in 8:1; 9:10, 24 (see also 7:6).

Whether the king accepts Haman's offer is unclear. It is possible to interpret 3:11 to indicate that the king declined to accept payment and authorized
the destruction of the Jews gratis. But it is also possible, with Moore, to translate the first part of the king's response as, "Well, it's your money," and to draw
an analogy to Genesis 23, in which Ephron the Hittite at first declines Abraham's offer to pay for the cave of Machpelah (vv. 11, 15) but in the end receives the money nonetheless (v. 16).[124] In support of the latter option, one can
cite Esther's claim that "we have been *sold*—I and my people—to be destroyed, slain, and annihilated" (7:4; emphasis added; cf. the selling of Joseph
in Gen. 37:25–28). Either way, it is revealing that the king mentions the money
first and the people only second and is satisfied to delegate a decision even of
such gravity to an enemy of the Jews (3:11).

3. The Edict
of Genocide Is Issued (3:12–13)

3:12 In the first month, on the thirteenth day, the king's scribes were summoned and, in accordance with all that Haman had directed, a writ was
drawn up and issued to all the king's satraps and to the governors of each
province and to the officials of every people, to each province in its own
script and to every people in its own language. It was drawn up in the
name of King Ahasuerus and sealed with his signet. 13 Letters were dispatched by couriers to all the king's provinces with instructions to destroy, slay, and annihilate all the Jews—young and old, women and children—on a single day, the thirteenth of the twelfth month (that is, the
month of Adar), and to take their property as plunder.

[124]Moore, *Esther*, 40.

The day on which the genocidal royal order is issued (3:12) is precisely eleven months before the day on which it is to be put into effect (8:12; 9:1, 17). This is a date fraught with irony, as this is also the day before Passover (see Exod. 12:6; Lev. 23:5), the festival that celebrates the triumph of the Jews over their oppressors. Perhaps Haman and his cohorts relied again upon astrological considerations: in some Babylonian texts, the *shapattu,* the date of the full moon (in the middle of the lunar month) was thought to be a time of good omen.[125] If so, they drastically misplaced their trust, for "the reverse occurred" (9:1), and the dynamic of redemption associated with Passover reappeared precisely when genocide had been expected.

The language that repeats the issuance of this second royal edict (3:12) is strikingly close to the language that reported the issuance of the first, which required "that each man shall be master of his household and speak the language of his people" (1:22). Whereas the first edict seemed absurd and unenforceable, the second seems, in this post-Holocaust era, frighteningly realistic. The truth is, however, that full-scale genocide—that is, the annihilation of an entire ethnic group, wherever they are throughout an entire empire and without regard to their political or military status—is a Nazi innovation, lacking a strong precedent in the long, dreary history of human brutality and atrocity.[126] The edict that strikes us as fearful may have seemed foolish and even comical to the ancient audience, further evidence of Ahasuerus's and Haman's failure to grasp reality and to discharge their offices effectively. Their genocidal plan, of course, does not cease to be supremely wicked simply because it is unrealistic. In the Hebrew Bible generally, and in its wisdom literature particularly, folly and wickedness are not altogether distinguishable.

Who precisely performs the actions described in 3:12 is not specified, for the verbs are rendered in the passive voice. This conveys a sense of a vast, uncaring, faceless bureaucracy that relentlessly, deterministically pursues an agenda that no human mind has considered or reviewed in appropriate fashion.

It has been pointed out that "[t]he heaping up of synonyms [in 3:13] is in imitation of the legal style, and is common in Esther."[127] The effect in this instance is to emphasize the totality of the slaughter. The order "to take [the Jews'] property as plunder" is reminiscent of the Deuteronomic law about warfare with distant peoples, that is, nations other than the Canaanites (Deut. 20:10–15), but the order to slay the "women and children" fits the law about the Canaanites rather than that about the distant peoples (Deut. 20:16–18; cf.

---

[125]Roland de Vaux, *Ancient Israel,* New York, 1965, 2:476.

[126]See Steven T. Katz, *Historicism, the Holocaust, and Zionism,* New York, 1992. This is not to imply, however, that Haman's anti-Semitism had the racialist character of Nazism, an implication that would be totally anachronistic.

[127]Paton, 209.

1 Samuel 15, esp. vv. 8–9, 11–24). This gives the impression that Haman and Ahasuerus have initiated a holy war, but one seriously flawed, and in fact rendered unholy by the hope of material gain. In any event, the royal edict "to take [the Jews'] property as plunder" (Esth. 3:13) stands in marked contrast to the thrice-repeated report that the Jews themselves, when the situation reversed, "did not lay a hand on the spoil" (9:10, 15, 16).

The Text of the Edict

Chapter B:1–7 (= Esther 13:1–7 in the Vulgate)

B:1 *The following is a copy of the letter:*

"The great king Artaxerxes writes to the satraps of the one hundred twenty-seven provinces from India to Ethiopia and to the governors subordinate to them as follows: 2 When I began to rule over many nations and to hold sway over the whole world, it was my wish not to be carried away by the overconfidence that comes from power but always to act equitably and gently, to provide my subjects with lives that are always tranquil, to make my empire humane and safe for travel to its very borders, and to restore the peace for which all men long. 3 When I inquired of my counselors how this might be brought about, a man who is outstanding among us for his sound judgment, constant in his good will, and who has proven himself by his firm faithfulness and gained the second rank in the kingdom, Haman, 4 brought a point to our attention: mixed in with all the races of the empire, there is a certain people of ill-will whose laws set it against every other people and who regularly disregard the decrees of kings, so that the unified administration that has been irreproachably designed by ourselves cannot be put into effect.

5 "Having understood that this unique nation is continually in opposition to all men, maintains a way of life that is foreign and based on alien laws, is inimical to our interests and commits the worst offenses, so that the stability of the empire cannot be realized, 6 we therefore decree that all those designated in the documents drawn up by Haman, who is in charge of the administration and a second father to us, shall, together with their wives and children, be utterly destroyed by the swords of their enemies, without pity or compassion, on the fourteenth day of the twelfth month, Adar, of the current year. 7 These persons who have so long been full of ill-will shall descend into the netherworld by a violent death on the same day in order that they may henceforth leave our affairs stable and undisturbed."

Chapter B, the second of the six "Additions to Esther" from the "Apocrypha" (see commentary on chapter A), interrupts the natural progression from 3:13 to 3:14; in the MT, 3:12–15 should be read as a unit. Chapter B is written in a very elegant and florid Greek, a feature it shares only with chap. E, the text of the counter-edict. It is therefore most probable that it was originally composed in Greek and not translated from a lost Hebrew or Aramaic text, as may well be the case with some of the other Additions. Since its point is to specify the contents of the writ mentioned in 3:12, the chapter can be most fruitfully compared with other instances in which royal proclamations of various sorts have been incorporated into narrative (e.g., Ezra 1:2–4; 4:17–22; 6:3–12; 7:11–28). Indeed, it is conceivable that the existence of these texts attributed to Persian kings (which themselves may not always be authentic) stimulated the composition of chap. B. But as Moore points out, the closest parallel actually lies in a Jewish book probably from the first century B.C.E., a book whose affinities with Esther are multiple and unlikely to be coincidental. This is the letter of King Ptolemy Philopater in 3 Macc. 3:12–29, in which the Hellenistic monarch decrees the annihilation of the Jews of Alexandria.[128]

The letter of the Persian king (called Artaxerxes, as always in the LXX) presents him as an idealistic, reasonable, and rather philosophical monarch, possessed of great eloquence. Needless to say, his acceptance of his vicegerent's call for the destruction of all Jews in his empire, "without pity or compassion" (B:6–7), belies the attempt to paint him in such positive tones. Indeed, Haman is presented as "outstanding . . . for his sound judgment, constant in his good will, and [one] who has proven himself by his firm faithfulness" (v. 3). This would put things in a different light if we did not know that the evil decree was drawn up "in accordance with all that Haman had directed" (3:12). "[T]hus as Soubigou has sarcastically observed: 'The eulogy of Haman was by Haman.' "[129] The effect of this public relations document is, not surprisingly, to change certain critical features of the MT to the benefit of the king and especially his prime minister. Thus the Jews are presented as not only disobedient and possessed of a different set of laws (as in 3:8), but misanthropic as well (B:4), and impeding the emergence of stability and right order in the empire (B:5). This charge of misanthropy is of a piece with certain currents in Greco-Roman anti-Judaism and would alone serve to establish chap. B as a late interpolation.

The date for the pogrom, the fourteenth of Adar (B:6), conforms to the date given elsewhere in the Greek version, though not with the MT, which consistently reads the thirteenth of the same month.

---

[128]Carey A. Moore, *Daniel, Esther, and Jeremiah: The Additions,* AB, Garden City, N.Y., 1977, 191, 195–99 (hereafter this volume will be referred to as Moore, *Additions*).

[129]Ibid., 193. The reference is to L. Soubigou, *Esther traduit et commente,* 2d ed., Bible de Jérusalem, Paris, 1952, 680.

3. The Edict of Genocide
Is Issued (continued) (3:14–15)

3:14 A copy of the writ was to be issued as a decree in every province and publicly displayed to all the peoples, so that they might be ready for that day. 15 The couriers went out posthaste at the king's command, and the decree was issued in the fortified compound of Susa. The king and Haman sat down to drink, but the city of Susa was thrown into confusion.

In the MT, 3:14–15 is the continuation of 3:12–13 and should be read without regard to the later interpolation of chap. B. The clause "so that they might be ready for that day" (v. 14) turns out to be immensely ironic and not a little comical, since that for which the anti-Semites must ready themselves is their own annihilation, itself the result of the next royal edict (8:9–9:19). Perhaps v. 14 is deliberately phrased in such a way that what the king orders is not the destruction of the Jews, but readiness for the day alone.[130]

Chapter 3:15 draws a contrast between two parts of Susa, the fortified compound in which the royal residences are found and the city in which the populace live. The structure of the verse conveys a sense of dizzying action. It consists of four short clauses,[131] each beginning (atypically for biblical Hebrew) with a noun followed by a verb in the perfect. Ahasuerus and Haman's sitting down for drinks (the meaning is probably another full banquet) contrasts with the "confusion" that reigns outside the fortified compound, intensifying our sense of their crassness and amorality. Retrospectively, it recalls nothing so much as Joseph's brothers sitting down to eat a meal just after throwing him into a pit from which they never expected him to emerge alive (Gen. 37:25). Prospectively, Ahasuerus and Haman's drinking foreshadows the partying of the Jews on the first Purim and on every anniversary of it (Esth. 9:16–19). This is even more the case if we follow Paton's suggestion to "translate *banquet* instead of *drink,* regarding the verb as a denominative from the word 'banquet' [*mišteh*], lit. 'drinking.' "[132]

Precisely why the city of Susa is thrown into "confusion" (3:15) is unclear. Perhaps it is only because of the furious activity emanating from the royal compound and the bizarre edict to be ready for the day nearly a year later when the Jews are to be annihilated. Perhaps it is only the Jews who are thrown into "confusion" as they contemplate what must seem an inevitable demise.[133]

---

[130]Hakham, 27.
[131]Ibid., 28.
[132]Paton, 211.
[133]See Ehrlich, 116, and Rashi and Ibn Ezra *ad loc.*

Close attention to the end of the tale, however, suggests a third possibility: it may be that the Susan Gentiles were severely distressed at the thought that their streets would flow with the blood of the Jews who had been living peacefully in their midst. It must not be overlooked (for it often has been) that the enemies of the Jews in Esther are a circumscribed subgroup of the imperial population and do not include the provincial officers, the satraps, or other royal officials in their number (see, e.g., 9:1–4). The book of Esther does not present Gentiles as inveterately or even generally anti-Jewish or the Jews as inherently set against the populace of the host culture.

IV. Mordecai Persuades Esther to Intercede with the King

Esther 4:1–17

1. Esther's Ignorance and Resistance (4:1–11)

4:1 When Mordecai found out all that had happened, he rent his garments, put on sackcloth and ashes, and went through the city, crying loudly and bitterly. 2 He came only as far as the palace gate, for it was forbidden to enter the palace gate dressed in sackcloth. (3 In every province, wherever the king's command and decree had reached, there was great mourning among the Jews, with fasting, weeping, and wailing, and the whole community lay in sackcloth and ashes.) 4 When Esther's maidens and eunuchs came and told her, she was extremely agitated. She sent clothing for Mordecai to wear so that he could take off his sackcloth, but he would not accept it. 5 Then Esther summoned Hathach, one of the king's eunuchs whom he had appointed to serve her, and ordered him to find out what was the matter with Mordecai and what this was all about. 6 Hathach went out to Mordecai in the city square in front of the palace gate, 7 and Mordecai told him all that had happened to him and the story[a] of the money that Haman had offered to deposit in the royal treasury in exchange for the destruction of the Jews. 8 He also gave him a copy of the decree for their destruction that had been issued in Susa so that he might show it to Esther, and inform her, and charge her to go to the king to beg for his mercy and to entreat him on behalf of her people. 9 Hathach came and reported to Esther what Mordecai had said, 10 and Esther then instructed Hathach to give Mordecai this message: 11 "All the king's courtiers and the population of the king's provinces know that if any man

or woman enters the king's presence in the inner court without having
been summoned, there is but one law for him—to be put to death, unless
the king extends the golden scepter to him so that he may live. As for
myself, I have not been summoned to enter the king's presence now for
thirty days."

a. Many commentators translate *pārāšâ,* as "exact amount," or the like,[134] on the basis of the form of the same root with the meaning, "make distinct, clarify" (e.g., Lev.
24:12). This yields good sense here, but not in the only other biblical attestation of the
word, 10:2. Our translation "story" fits both 10:2 and a postbiblical usage of the identical noun in the sense of "text, passage."

With chap. 4, the focus shifts away from the lethal machinations at court
and onto Mordecai's efforts to thwart them. These efforts begin with Mordecai's engaging in well-attested rites of mourning, tearing his clothes, donning
sackcloth, putting on ashes, and wailing publicly (4:1). In ancient Israel, "these
rites . . . were believed to be efficacious in turning away the divine wrath."[135]
In Esther, the mention of them and of fasting later in the same chapter (vv. 3
and 16) is as close to traditional religious practice as the book of Esther ever
gets, and some have thought that they here serve only as conventional expressions of grief or as a way to capture the queen's attention, rather than as theur-
gic performances. As the story develops, however, a marvelous set of coincidences does indeed reverse the apparently hopeless plight of the Jews, and it
is best to think that the author wants us to suspect that this was indeed partially
in response to the extraordinary penitential exercises of Mordecai, Esther, and
the rest of the Jewish people.

Esther 4:3 interrupts the account of Mordecai's public mourning to tell us
that the Jews throughout the empire were engaging in the same sort of rites. It
has been plausibly suggested that this verse would be better placed at the end
of chap. 3.[136] In its present position, however, it does serve to underscore
Mordecai's status as the prototypical and preeminent Jew: He knows of the plot
and reacts to it before his fellow Jews do. He is their representative at court, in
the very nerve center of the hostile forces, and if they are to be delivered, it will
be as a consequence of his initiative.

Esther 4:4 also poses problems. How Mordecai knows of the plot when Esther, much closer to the seat of power, does not is one mystery. Another involves the knowledge that Esther's staff obviously have of her relationship to
Mordecai when her Jewishness itself is still a secret. In any event, given her
ignorance of the cause of his public mourning, her extreme agitation would

[134]E.g., Paton, 217.
[135]Paton, 214.
[136]E.g., Ehrlich, 116.

seem to be the result not of the genocidal decree against her people, but of her embarrassment at his grossly inappropriate appearance amid the opulence of the fortified compound of Susa. Perhaps she is also discomfited by the thought that Mordecai's public demonstration of his Jewishness will eventually undermine her own persona as a Gentile queen. The effect of vv. 4–11 is thus to highlight the distance between Mordecai the Jew and Esther the Persian. A critique of Jews who fail to identify with their people may be implied here (cf. 3 Macc. 7:10–12).

Esther 4:5 highlights another contrast between Mordecai and Esther, his knowledge (*yd'*, v. 1) versus her ignorance (*yd'*, v. 5). The royal eunuch Hathach finds Mordecai in the city square, a place often associated with rites of lamentation (v. 6; cf. Isa. 15:3; Jer. 48:38). There Mordecai tells him "all that had happened *to him*" (Esth. 4:7; emphasis added), perhaps signaling the Jew's acknowledgment that he was the cause of the impending catastrophe.[137] But it is also possible that we have here another of Mordecai's identifications with his people: He is their representative, even their personification, and what happens to them happens to him—for ill, as here, or for good, as at the end of the tale.

Mordecai's mention of Haman's bribe in 4:7 is rhetorically powerful and serves to underscore our sense of him as a master tactician. As Paton observes, "Mordecai shrewdly calculates that [the] buying of the Jews will rouse Esther's wrath more than anything else."[138] The mention of the astronomical sum that Haman is prepared to pay in order to obliterate the Jews will give her a chilling sense of the degree of Haman's hatred.

Mordecai's charge to Esther to go to the king ". . . to entreat him on behalf of her people" (4:8) invites an analogy with the role of Moses in the book of Exodus. Esther is to Ahasuerus as Moses is to Pharaoh (cf. Exod. 7:1–2).[139] The timing of Purim, which comes a month before Passover, may in part account for this and other similarities between the two narratives. The differences, however, must also be faced, not the least of which is this: Whereas Moses (and Aaron) fail to persuade Pharaoh (partly because of God's predetermination; Exod. 7:3–5), whom God must therefore compel to release the Israelites, Esther (and Mordecai) succeed through their own wit and courage and an astonishing set of benign coincidences, which may also reflect divine action.

Esther's hesitation to heed her guardian's command (4:11) is another analogy to the early chapters of Exodus, when Moses repeatedly tries to avoid his momentous commission (Exod. 3:11; 4:10, 13; 6:12, 30; esp. 10:28, where Pharaoh decrees that Moses shall die on the day he next sees the king's face).[140]

---

[137]Thus, Hakham, 31.
[138]Paton, 217.
[139]Gerleman, 105.
[140]Ibid., 106.

The rule that one enters the Persian king's presence unsummoned only upon pain of death is also attested in Herodotus,[141] though with the important proviso that individuals could request an audience. Why Esther does not immediately do so—she had nearly a year until the fateful day—is not told us. But the way the narrative stands surely enhances the dramatic tension, as Esther is now called upon to risk not only her royal office (the deposition of her predecessor Vashti is surely on her mind) but also her very life, all on behalf of the beleaguered people with whom she has not yet publicly identified. The notice about the death penalty for appearing before the king at one's own initiative is thus essential to the transformation of Esther from a beauty queen to a heroic savior, and from a self-styled Persian to a reconnected Jew. The author has enhanced the dramatic effect of Esth. 4:11 by the shift to direct address,[142] a move that fits with the more personal and plaintive tone of the content of her message to Mordecai.

2. Esther Accepts
Her Providential Role (4:12–17)

4:12 When Esther's words were reported to Mordecai, **13** Mordecai sent this message back to Esther: "Don't imagine that you alone of all the Jews will escape because you are in the king's palace. **14** On the contrary, if you really do remain silent in such a time as this, relief and deliverance will arise for the Jews from another quarter, but you and your father's family will perish. And who knows? Perhaps it is for just such an occasion as this that you have attained to royal estate!" **15** Then Esther sent this answer back to Mordecai: **16** "Go, assemble all the Jews to be found in Susa and fast for me: neither eat nor drink for three days, night and day, and I and my maidens shall likewise fast. After that, I will go to the king, although it is against the law. And if I perish, I perish!" **17** So Mordecai passed [through the city] and did all that Esther had enjoined upon him.

In this key section of the narrative, the intermediary Hathach has disappeared, and we are left with the tense debate between Esther and Mordecai, which results in her acceptance of the life-threatening mission to save the Jews from annihilation. In Esth. 4:13–14, Mordecai seeks to call his cousin back to her Jewish roots. She must not allow her queenship to go to her head. When matters become difficult for the Jews, she (like Moses) will prove unable to avoid identification with the imperiled nation of exiles. Precisely why she and

---

[141]Herodotus 1:99; 3:72, 77, 84, 118, 140.
[142]Moore, *Esther,* 49.

her father's family will perish if she sits out the crisis is unclear; too much pursuit of precision is unwise for the exegete when the text is so vague. Probably Mordecai means simply to let Esther know that Haman and his anti-Jewish cohorts will eventually discover her real identity and prevail upon the ever malleable Ahasuerus to hand her over for execution. Here, too, we may hear overtones of the critique of Jews who were "passing," as some sought to do in the Second Temple period, especially under the pressures of Hellenization (e.g., Jub. 15:33–34; 3 Macc. 7:10–12), and as many have sought to do in the modern West, especially under the pressures of democratization and secularization.

The identity of "another quarter" from which "relief and deliverance will arise for the Jews" if Esther is silent is unclear (Esth. 4:14). It is conceivable that all Mordecai means is that he will in that case devise another stratagem to rescue the Jews, with the exception of his high-placed and uncooperative cousin. The end of v. 14, however, suggests a different and deeper interpretation: Esther's astonishing rise to the queenship may reflect a providential plan for Jewish succor, and it would be folly to imagine that one person's noncompliance could derail the entire plan. In support of this more theological reading, the expression "who knows" (*mî yôdēa‘*) is suggestive. In several other passages in the Hebrew Bible, these words preface a guarded hope that penitential practice may induce God to relent from his harsh decree, granting deliverance where destruction had been expected (cf. 2 Sam. 12:22; Joel 2:14; and Jonah 3:9). If this is the background to the usage in Esth. 4:14, then we have here another echo of the rites of lamentation with which the chapter began. And if "another quarter" is God, then we have in this verse the strongest approximation in the Masoretic Esther to an explicit theological affirmation.

In the Alpha Text version of the same exchange, there is no analogy to the MT's theological reticence. "If you neglect your people by failing to come to their aid," Mordecai admonishes Esther, "God will be their aid and their deliverance . . . " (AT 5:9). If, as has been argued,[143] the AT predates the MT, we may have in the latter a deliberate attempt to mute the robust theological affirmation of the former and to substitute a more delicate and ambiguous understanding of the ways of God. We cannot be sure, however, since how much of the current AT was available to the author/redactor of the MT is unknown. Esther's response in 4:16 displays a further maturation of her character. She now relies not upon her beauty, which would, in the absence of a miracle, be severely diminished after three days of fasting, but upon the penitential rites themselves and—though again, this is only implicit—upon God's gracious response to them. Whether she proposed to fast for all of each day is unknown; perhaps we are to imagine a fast during daylight only, as in the minor fasts of the Jewish liturgical calendar (including *Ta‘anit Esther,* "the Fast of Esther").

---

[143]See Fox, *Redaction.*

It is also possible that the expression "three days" is formulaic and not to be taken literally (cf. Gen. 22:4; Exod. 8:23; Hos. 6:2; Jonah 2:1; 3:3). Some scholars think the fast in v. 16 has an etiological character, and cite 9:31 in connection,[144] but this is not necessarily so (see the commentary on 9:31). In any event, the fast of Esther is of one and not three days' duration: it falls on the day before Purim (unless the holiday is celebrated on Sunday, in which case the fast falls on the previous Thursday), and it is of post-Talmudic origin in any case.

It is hard to know whether Esther's concluding words, "if I perish, I perish" (*ka'ăšer 'ābadtî 'ābādtî*, 4:16) reflect willing acceptance of her role or merely resignation to the death that will come either way, from Haman or from Ahasuerus. In either case, the words recall Jacob's when he reluctantly grants his ten sons permission to take his beloved youngest, Benjamin, to Egypt: "and if I am to be bereaved, I shall be bereaved" (*ka'ăšer šākōltî šākāltî*, Gen. 43:14). Given Esther's Benjaminite affiliation (Esth. 2:5) and the multiple connections of the book with the story of Joseph, this echo may be deliberate. Like Jacob, Esther, at considerable risk and pain, is accepting her role in the larger drama of Jewish salvation. The change in her character that has taken place in chap. 4 is subtly signaled by the end of its last verse. Now, instead of her doing Mordecai's bidding (as in 2:10, 20), he is doing Esther's bidding, relaying her instructions to the Jewish community (4:17). But there has also been a concomitant transformation in Esther's status. As Sidnie Ann White puts it, "[t]he powerless has become the powerful."[145] Esther has moved from being the adopted daughter of an exile, to the winner of a beauty contest, to the queen of Persia and Media, to the pivotal figure in the crisis hanging over the Jews, able to issue effective commands to her foster father.

Chapter 4 thus begins with Mordecai's mourning (vv. 1–2), expands to view the parallel ritual activity of the whole Jewish community (v. 3), and concludes, after some suspense and tense dialogue (vv. 4–14), with Esther's undertaking the same kind of ritual and agreeing to risk her life (as Mordecai has risked his) in order to save her endangered community (v. 15). Mordecai has won over Esther, and now it remains to be seen whether Esther can succeed in the more daunting challenge of winning over Ahasuerus. Who knows? Perhaps the rites have had an effect, and larger forces are at work that will rescue the Jews after all.

[144]E.g., Bardtke, 334.

[145]Sidnie Ann White, "Esther: A Feminine Model for Jewish Diaspora," in *Gender and Difference in Ancient Israel*, ed. Peggy L. Day, Minneapolis, 1989, 170.

Prayers of the Heroes

Chapter C:1–30 (= Esther 13:8–14:19 in the Vulgate)

1. Mordecai's Prayer (C:1–11)

c:1 *Recalling all the* LORD'*s deeds, he prayed to him,* 2 *saying: "*LORD, LORD, *almighty king, all things are in Your power, and none can oppose You when You want to rescue Israel,* 3 *for You made the heavens and the earth and every wondrous thing under heaven.* 4 *You are the* LORD *over everything, and there is none who can resist You, O* LORD.

5 *"You know all things. You know, O* LORD, *that it was not out of insolence or arrogance or the love of fame that I did this, not bowing down to the arrogant Haman,* 6 *for I would have been happy to kiss the soles of his feet in behalf of the rescue of Israel.* 7 *Rather, I did this in order to avoid setting the glory of a man above the glory of God, and I shall bow to none but You, my* LORD, *and I shall not act out of arrogance.*

8 *"And now, O* LORD, *God, King, God of Abraham, spare Your people, for they are already eyeing our destruction and longing to annihilate the inheritance that was Yours from of old.* 9 *Do not neglect Your portion, whom You redeemed for Yourself out of Egypt.* 10 *Hear my prayer, and have mercy on Your inheritance and turn our mourning into feasting, so that we may live to sing praises to Your name, O* LORD. *Do not allow the mouths that praise You to be obliterated!"*

11 *And all Israel cried out with all their strength, for their own death was staring them in the eye.*[a]

a. Literally, "their death was in their eyes."

In essence, chap. C consists of two well-wrought prayers, the first that of Mordecai, the second of Esther. Mordecai's prayer consists of three elements: praise of God the omnipotent (vv. 2–4), a defense of his own motivation in refusing to bow to Haman (vv. 5–7), and a petition for God to intervene on behalf of his people and portion in their moment of mortal danger (vv. 8–10). The first and the last of these elements are quite familiar from the Hebrew Bible, especially the book of Psalms, and figure prominently in the devotional literature of the Second Temple period (to which the entire chapter exhibits several verbal parallels). Mordecai's defense, though also displaying familiar language, is more interesting in that it seeks to parry the charge that it was his pride alone that brought the calamitous circumstances upon his people. The defense does this by supplying a point of information left tantalizingly unspecified in chap. 3—the reason for Mordecai's refusal to bow to Haman (see commentary to 3:1–6). He did this, we are now told, not out of arrogance, but out of religious scruple, lest he "[set] the glory of a man above the glory of God" (C:7). This puts Mordecai's actions into the praiseworthy category of resistance to idolatry, a pressing issue in late Second Temple literature (cf., for example, Daniel 3, esp. vv. 17–18, and Daniel 4, esp. vv. 22–24) and always a problem for Jews living under an alien religious order.

The Greek diction and style in chapter C suggest that it may be a translation from a Semitic text. In fact, an Aramaic parallel to Mordecai's prayer in C:2–10 has been found in the Vatican Library.[146] C:2–10 should be viewed as a Jewish interpolation into an older form of the book of Esther for the purpose of making Mordecai more conventionally religious and clearing his good name from the suspicion of arrogance. The religious feeling behind the prayer is no less the moving for this, and the urgency of the situation is communicated most effectively.

2. Esther's Prayer (C:12–30)

C:12 *Queen Esther, seized by the anguish of death, fled to the* LORD. 13 *Taking off her splendid robes, she put on the robes of distress and mourning, and in place of her magnificent ointments, she covered her head with ashes and dung and debased her body severely. Every place that she had rejoiced to adorn, she now covered with dishevelled hair.*

14 *Then she entreated the* LORD, *God of Israel, saying:*

"My LORD, *You alone are our king. Help me who am alone and have no help but You,* 15 *for I am taking my life in my hands.*[a] 16 *From my earliest childhood in my family's tribe, I have been hearing that You,* LORD, *took Israel from all the nations, and their fathers from all their ancestors, as an everlasting heritage and that You did for them just as You had promised.* 17 *But now, we have sinned against You, and You have handed us over to our enemies* 18 *because we gave glory to their gods. Just You are, O* LORD. 19 *But now, not satisfied to have us in bitter servitude, they*

---

[146]See J. M. Fuller, "The Rest of the Chapters of the Book of Esther," in *Apocrypha of the Speaker's Commentary,* ed. Henry Wace, London, 1888, 385. Fuller's translation can also be found in Moore, *Additions,* 205–6.

have joined hands with their idols **20** *to annul the utterance of Your own mouth, to obliterate Your inheritance, to stop the mouths of those who praise You, to extinguish the glory of Your house and Your altar,* **21** *and to open the mouths of the nations in order to acclaim the virtues of idols, and to worship a fleshly king forever.* **22** *Do not, O LORD, hand over Your scepter to those who do not exist, and let them not laugh at our downfall. Instead, turn their plot against themselves, and make him who began this against us into an example.*

23 *"Be mindful, O LORD. Reveal Yourself in the moment of our affliction, and give me courage, king of the gods and ruler over every power!* **24** *Put the appropriate words into my mouth in the presence of the lion and turn his heart to hatred of the one who is fighting against us so that he and those who think like him may come to an end.* **25** *Rescue us by Your power, and help me, who am alone and have no one but You, O LORD.*

"You have knowledge of all things. **26** *You know that I hate the pomp of the lawless and abhor the bed of the uncircumcised or of any foreigner.* **27** *You know the constraint upon me, that I abhor the symbol of my lofty position which is on my head when I am seen in public. I abhor it like a menstruous rag, and I do not wear it in private.* **28** *Your servant has never dined at Haman's table, nor have I extolled the king's banquet or drunk the wine of libations.* **29** *From the day my status changed until now, Your servant has not delighted in any but You, O LORD, God of Abraham.* **30** *O God, whose power prevails over all, listen to the voice of those who are without hope, and rescue us from the hand of the wicked. And deliver me from my fear!"*

a. Literally, "my peril is in my hand."

Queen Esther's prayer is reminiscent of Mordecai's in C:2–10 both in wording and in concept. In essence, it divides into two sections. The first (vv. 14–25a) is an elaborate effort to persuade the just God to come to the aid of a sinful, idolatrous people. Appealing to the honor and the reputation—perhaps even the ego—of the jealous God, Esther points out that Israel's current oppressors have gone beyond the "bitter servitude" (v. 19) that the chosen people are traditionally said to have merited in recompense for sin. The new oppressors now are seeking to obliterate them altogether. This would nullify God's own pledged word, deprive him of his palace (the Temple) and of the gifts offered him there, leave him without worshipers, give the idols an ostensible victory, and vindicate emperor-worship at the expense of monotheism. In short, if the LORD is truly a jealous God, he must not punish Israel's idolatry so severely that it causes the nations that do not know him to exult in triumph (cf., e.g., Deut. 32:27–31).

In Esth. C:23–25, the queen moves from her people to herself, asking for divine assistance in her appointed task of persuading the king to counteract Haman's plot. Verses 25b–30 closely resemble vv. 5–7, in which Mordecai defends himself against the suspicion of arrogance and insists that only monotheistic scruple accounts for his refusal to bend the knee to Haman. In Esther's case, the charge to be parried is that she enjoys the luxury of court and the eminence of her queenly status and that she willingly sleeps with a Gentile, eats forbidden foods, and drinks forbidden wine. Perhaps the exchange with Mordecai in chap. 4, when Esther tries to get him to take off his sackcloth (v. 4), has prompted this apologetic response, with its pointed insistence that Esther never broke faith with her God or her people. From the MT one cannot ascertain whether this is so; chap. 4 certainly leaves the possibility open that Esther had once defected, only to return to her Jewish identification upon Mordecai's presenting her with evidence of the enormity of Haman's plan. One effect of C:25b–30 is thus to retroject the heroic Esther even into chap. 2, in which she becomes queen. Esther's consistency of devotion is purchased at the expense of dramatic tension and character development. Another effect of all of C:12–30 is shared by most of the six "Additions to Esther"—to make a theologically ambiguous story into a clear and univocal example of the power of conventional piety. Esther has been transformed into a self-consciously loyal Jewess, a woman of prayer, penitence, and religious observance, in bed and at table. So have Jews tended to perceive her ever since, even though they themselves lost the "Additions to Esther."

Esther Confronts the King

Chapter D:1–16 (= Esther 15:1–16 in the Vulgate)

D:1 *On the third day, when she had finished praying, she took off the garments of a supplicant and put on splendid attire.* 2 *After calling upon the all-seeing God and deliverer, she became utterly radiant, and took two maids with her,* 3 *leaning daintily on the one for support* 4 *while the other followed, bearing her train.* 5 *She blushed with the perfection of her beauty, and her face was joyous and pleasing, though her heart tightened with fear.*

6 *Having passed through all the portals, she stood face to face with the king. He was seated upon his royal throne and clothed in all his splendid apparel, and all covered with gold and precious gems inspiring great fear.* 7 *Raising his face, ablaze with the most intense anger, he looked at her. The queen staggered, changed color, became faint, and leaned upon*

the head of the maid who was walking in front of her. **8** *But God changed the king's spirit to gentleness, and, in great distress, he sprang from his throne and took her in his arms until she revived. He comforted her with soothing words.* **9** *"What is it, Esther?" he said. "I am your brother. Take heart!* **10** *You shall not die, for this decree of ours applies only to the general public.* **11** *Come near!"* **12** *Then, raising his golden scepter, he tapped her neck, hugged her, and said, "Speak to me."*

13 *"My Lord," she answered, "I saw You like an angel of God, and my heart was troubled with fear of Your glorious appearance.* **14** *For You inspire awe, My Lord, though Your face is full of kindness."* **15** *As she was speaking, she collapsed and fainted.* **16** *The king became alarmed, and all his attendants tried to comfort her.*

Chapter D is an expansion of 5:1–2; in the LXX it precedes 5:3, not 5:1, as in our translation, which is based on the MT but includes the six Septuagintal "Additionᵉ to Esther." The reference to Esther's finishing her prayer in D:1 evidences continuity with chap. C, and the two chapters may well come from the same hand.

Chapter D heightens in baroque fashion the drama of Esther's uninvited approach to the king. Everything is here pushed to the extreme, in contrast to the concise and understated style of the MT. Having doffed her clothes of mourning (see C:13), which she donned in repudiation of her stately office and in identification with her downtrodden kinsmen, Esther now puts on "splendid attire," becoming "utterly radiant," "blush[ing] with the perfection of her beauty" (D:1–2, 5). Similarly, the king's attire "inspire[s] great fear," and he is, to boot, "ablaze with the most intense anger" (vv. 6–7). As in an overwrought Romantic novel, Esther feels faint and nearly passes out, so intense is the challenge she faces (v. 7). What rescues her is, first, God's intervention, miraculously transforming the king's spirit from blazing anger to courtly gentleness, and, second, the king himself, who (again in baroque or Romantic fashion) "sprang from his throne and took her in his arms until she revived" from her swoon (v. 8)— though she afterward "collapsed and fainted" anyway (v. 15).

The effect of chap. D is twofold. First, it again puts the *megillah* into an explicitly theistic framework, ascribing to God events that are therein never explicitly interpreted in theological fashion, though there are subtle suggestions that such an interpretation is indeed appropriate. Second, chap. D enhances the image of Esther herself by concentrating on the magnitude of the challenge she faces. Whereas the MT has Esther winning the king's grace as soon as he sees her (5:2), D:6–7 has rewritten the story so as to show him "inspiring great fear" and "ablaze with the most intense anger." Yet Esther, though she staggers, does not retreat and, with God's crucial help, presses ahead in her mission of Jewish deliverance—all without any further counsel from Mordecai. (The greater individuality and heroism that the Additions confer upon Esther herself give the lie, incidentally, to any claim that the Hebrew Bible was more appreciative of women than the ongoing Jewish tradition.)

The style of chap. D indicates substantial influence from the tradition of the Hellenistic novel. The closest parallel, however, is to be found in a Jewish work quite similar to Esther—the book of Judith—especially in its account of Judith's initial approach to the Assyrian general, Holofernes (Judith 10:1–11:4). Esther (as she appears in the Septuagint and the rabbinic tradition) and Judith are both celebrated for their reliance on God, their religious observance, their faithfulness to the ways of the ancestors, their courage, their gift of persuasive speech, and their physical beauty. It is reasonable to infer that these two heroines reflect an ideal of womanhood widespread in late Second Temple Judaism.

V. Esther Approaches the King and Asks for Two Banquets

Esther 5:1–14

1. The King Grants Her Requests (5:1–8)

5:1 On the third day, Esther donned her royal robes and stood in the inner courtyard of the king's palace, facing the king's palace, while the king was sitting upon his royal throne in the throne room, facing the entrance of the palace. 2 When the king caught sight of Queen Esther standing in the courtyard, she won his grace. The king extended the golden scepter that he held in his hand to Esther, and Esther drew near and touched the head of the scepter. 3 The king said to her, "What is bothering you, Queen Esther, and what is your request? Up to half the empire— it shall be granted to you!" 4 "If it please Your Majesty," Esther replied, "let Your Majesty and Haman come today to a banquet that I have prepared for You." 5 The king said, "Get Haman here fast so that Esther's wish may be fulfilled," and the king and Haman came to the feast that Esther had prepared.

6 At the wine feast, the king said to Esther, "What is your wish? It shall be granted to you! What is your request? Up to half the empire—it shall be fulfilled!" 7 Esther answered, "My wish and my request . . . 8 If I have won Your Majesty's favor and if it please Your Majesty to grant my wish

and to fulfill my request, let Your Majesty and Haman come to the banquet that I will prepare for them—and tomorrow I will do as Your Majesty has said."

Whereas Esther had feared that the king's reaction to her uninvited appearance would be lethal to her (4:11), she, in fact, wins his grace (*nāśā' ḥēn*, 5:2), just as she had won his grace (*nāśā' ḥēn wāḥesed*) in the beauty contest by which she became queen (2:17) and had earlier won the grace of everyone who saw her (*nāśā' ḥēn*, 2:15). All this, it will be remembered, was in large part owing to the mysterious charm she first exerted (*nāśā' ḥesed*) upon the harem-keeper Hegai, who, in consequence, supplied her with cosmetics and other advantages over the other contestants (2:9). If Esther's intercession occurs immediately at the conclusion of the three-day fast (4:16), and if the fast immediately followed the issuance of the genocidal decree on the thirteenth of the first month (3:12), then she approached Ahasuerus during Passover (Lev. 23:5–6)—a most auspicious date for the Jews. Note the parallel of Esth. 5:2 with Exod. 12:36, which reports that the LORD put the people in favor (*ḥēn*) with the Egyptians.

The Talmudic authority Rabbi Hanina interpreted the absence of any word for robes in the Hebrew to 5:1 (literally, "Esther donned royalty") to mean that the Holy Spirit clothed her so that she spoke through prophetic inspiration.[147] Within the context of the book of Esther itself, this is inaccurate, of course, but it does capture the sense of the text that a mysterious grace envelops Esther as she risks her life for her people, winning the favor of the irascible king whose rules she has just been discovered breaking. Esther 5:1 nicely conveys the magnitude of the authority she challenges by using the root of the word for king (*mlk*) fully six times.[148] But one of these is in the notice that "Esther donned her royal robes [*malkût*]," which may signal her acceptance of Mordecai's challenge that "[p]erhaps it is for just such an occasion as this that you have attained to royal estate [*malkût*]" (4:14).[149] If so, in 5:1 we see Esther the beauty queen giving way to Esther the true queen, willing to intercede with the king to prevent an unnecessary killing.

At first it seems that in approaching the king unbidden, Esther is defying his command (4:11), thus repeating Vashti's crime (1:12) and confirming Haman's charge that the Jews are insubordinate (3:8). The wording of 5:1–2 makes, however, the opposite point: Esther enters only the courtyard and awaits the king's invitation before approaching the throne.[150] The scene in our

---

[147]*b. Meg.* 15a, by analogy with 1 Chron. 12:19.

[148]Bardtke, 336.

[149]Fox, *Character,* 68.

[150]Contra Mieke Bal, "Lots of Writing," *Semeia* 54 (1991): 92, who writes that "[Vashti] is eliminated only to reemerge in Esther, who takes her place, avenging punishment by turning disobedience into access to power."

passage actually conforms to the topos that Larry L. Lyke calls the "woman with a cause," in which a wise and eloquent woman approaches a king in hopes of having justice done. In the cases most analogous to ours, the woman acts to avert a killing inevitable in the absence of royal intervention—Abigail, for example, pleading with David not to shed Nabal's blood needlessly (1 Sam. 25:24–31) or the wise woman of Tekoa pleading, again with David, to save the life of her murderer son, actually David's own murderer son Absalom (2 Sam. 14:4–17).[151] Given the force of these antecedents and the greater magnitude of the killing that Esther seeks to avert, it is odd that all she now requests—though the king offers her "up to half the empire" (Esth. 5:3)—is the king's and Haman's presence at a banquet. There are several ways of explaining this. It may be that she wants the king to have forgotten her sin of uninvited entry before she makes her request.[152] Or perhaps Queen Esther wants to delay until such time as the king, under the influence of wine, is in a good mood and willing to comply with her wishes.[153] Since early rabbinic times, Jewish commentators have often thought the idea is to make Ahasuerus jealous of Haman—Why should the queen be so eager to have him at her party?—and thus predisposed to grant her request to do him and his hate-filled cohorts in.[154] Whatever Esther's motive, it cannot be doubted that the ensuing banquet scenes impart a dramatic intensity to the tale that otherwise would be wanting, had she simply accused Haman at this, her first opportunity. And by seeming to honor Haman, she fattens him for the kill, for now he goes out elated at being invited to sup with the royal couple, full of his own—very transient!—importance (5:9–12).

With the king's immediate acquiescence (5:5), Esther is now successfully stage-managing the scene, commanding both Ahasuerus and Haman just as she successfully commanded Mordecai at the end of the previous chapter (4:15–17). It is unclear whether the words "so that Esther's wish may be fulfilled" in 5:5 are part of the king's order or the narrator's comment on the action. If they are the former, then Ahasuerus now subordinates Haman to Esther, just as he will subordinate Haman to Mordecai in the next chapter (6:6–11) and will award the anti-Semite's estate to Esther after his execution (8:1).

It seems odd that Esther's only request at the banquet is that there should be another banquet of the same threesome (5:7). Perhaps v. 7 should be inter-

---

[151]Larry L. Lyke, " 'And the two of them struggled in the field': Intertextuality and the Interpretation of the *Mashal* of the Wise Woman of Tekoa in 2 Samuel 14:1–20," Ph.D. diss., Harvard University, 1995, part 2.

[152]Eliezer Ashkenazi, *Yosef Leqaḥ*, in *Megillat Esther 'im Perush Ha-Gr"a Ha-Shalem*, ed. Chanan David Nobel, Jerusalem, 5752/1991, to Esther 5:4 (hereafter this volume will be identified as *Yosef Leqaḥ*).

[153]Elijah, Gaon of Vilna (see n. 152, above) to 5:4.

[154]See *b. Meg.* 15b; Rashi to 5:4, and Ehrlich, 118.

preted as indicating that Esther lost her nerve when she finally was in a position to point the finger at Haman. It may also be that her repetition of the words "wish and request" is simply the ancient Hebrew way of saying, "Yes." "Yes," Esther would then be saying, "I do have a wish and a request."[155] Either way, from the point of view of narrative technique, the delay builds up the suspense and guarantees that only on the third time that the king offers the queen whatever she wants "up to half the empire" will the climax come. As David Noel Freedman nicely puts it: "The third time is the charm in literary accounts. It is like the acrobat or magician who deliberately fails twice in trying to perform his most difficult feat, before succeeding on the third try."[156] The last clause of v. 8 would seem to mean that at the second banquet, Esther will indeed reveal her deepest wish. The die is cast, but it is not Haman's *pûr*!

2. Haman's Joy Turns
to Rage Again (5:9–14)

9 Haman went out that day joyful and merry. But when Haman saw that Mordecai in the king's gate neither rose nor stirred on his account, he became filled with rage against Mordecai. 10 But Haman controlled himself and went home. He then assembled his friends and his wife Zeresh, 11 and spoke to them about the greatness of his wealth and his many sons and all about how the king had promoted him and elevated him over the officials and royal courtiers. 12 "Not only that," Haman said, "but Queen Esther did not bring anyone to the banquet with the king that she made except me, and again tomorrow I am invited by her together with the king. 13 But all this is worth nothing to me whenever I see Mordecai the Jew sitting in the king's gate." 14 Then his wife Zeresh and all his friends said to him, "Let a stake be set up, fifty cubits high, and in the morning ask the king to have Mordecai impaled upon it. Then you can go with the king to the banquet joyfully." The proposal pleased Haman, and he had the stake set up.

This little passage nicely brings out both Haman's foolishness and his deviousness. His foolishness lies not only in his joy and merriment at the thought of the banquet that will, in fact, prove to be his downfall, but also in his inability to sustain any happiness and to suppress his anger when just one courtier refuses to pay him homage (v. 9). The expression "merry" (*ṭôb lēb*) has already occurred once before, in 1:10, where it describes Ahasuerus's mood just as he issues the fateful order to bring Vashti to the banquet. The use of this rare

---

[155]Moore, *Esther,* 57.
[156]Ibid., 58.

expression in these two contexts reinforces the similarity of Haman's character to Ahasuerus's and leads us to expect that here too the merriment is ill-considered and will be of short duration (cf. 1 Sam. 25:36). One of the themes of the book of Esther is the contrast between wise and foolish joy. Haman's joy is clearly foolish and transient, whereas that of the Jews, when events have at last gone their way (Esth. 8:16), turns out to be wise and enduring.

In fairness to Haman, Mordecai does seem to have escalated his noncompliance. Whereas before he had only refused to prostrate himself (3:2–5), now he neither rises nor stirs on account of the prime minister. Like Ahasuerus in the face of Vashti's noncompliance (1:12), Haman, for his part, flies into a rage (5:9). Why he does not take immediate action against the offender is not told us. His delay is reminiscent of Esther's requesting another banquet, rather than immediately fingering Haman, in the previous pericope (5:7–8). As Paton points out, in both cases, "[t]he author wishes to keep the reader in suspense as long as possible, and [in addition, here] to give Haman time to devise an exceptional penalty for Mordecai."[157] Haman's immediate response, to assemble his friends and his wife Zeresh, is a kind of comic inversion of Esther's action at the end of the previous chapter, where she orders Mordecai to assemble the Jewish community of Susa and to proclaim a public fast in her behalf (4:15–17). Whereas Esther overcomes her self-regard and acts to avert a slaughter, Haman acts out of self-regard that has become egomaniacal and is told to arrange yet another slaughter (5:14). That it is his wife who seems to take the lead in telling him what to do is ironic in the case of the prime minister of a king who has solemnly and irrevocably decreed "that each man shall be master of his household" (1:16–22). The connection of that decree with this advice is underscored by the common use of the words "the proposal pleased X" (*wayyîṭab haddābār bĕ‘ênê / lipnê*, 1:21 and 5:14). Though the conflict began as one between two men, Mordecai and Haman, it is now two women, Esther and Zeresh, who are determining the action.

There is also comedy in Haman's dissertating to his friends and his wife about his great success and lofty status (5:11). Is it conceivable that they do not know that he is a wealthy man and the prime minister? The point, of course, is that all this is unsatisfying so long as one courtier refuses to fall into line. And is his wife unaware that he has many sons? In just two verses (vv. 11–12), the narrator thus conveys a vivid image of a man with a profound inner weakness and a corollary need to concentrate upon externals. The false security of wealth is a common theme of wisdom literature, wherein reliance upon riches is characteristic of the fool (e.g., Prov. 11:28; 28:11), as are arrogance, false confidence, and hasty speech (e.g., Prov. 13:3; 14:16; 16:5; 27:1; 29:20)—all attributes that Haman exhibits in abundance in our passage. The verse from

---

[157]Paton, 238.

Proverbs that sounds as though it were composed with this passage in mind is best known in its King James rendering: "Pride *goeth* before destruction, and an haughty spirit before a fall" (Prov. 16:18).[158]

Haman's deviousness, also characteristic of the proverbial fool (e.g., Prov. 16:27–30), can be seen in Esth. 5:13, when he fails to mention that his real objection to Mordecai is the Jewish courtier's refusal to pay him homage. This verse has a strong affinity with 3:8, Haman's indictment of the Jews in general, wherein he also fails to mention Mordecai's slight of him (cf. "is worth nothing to me" [*'ênennû šōweh lî*], 5:13, with "it is not in Your Majesty's interest to leave them alone" [*lammelek 'ên šōweh lĕhannîhām*], 3:8). Once again Mordecai is the representative Jew, though it is unclear why Haman would not have thought him included in the coming genocide that he has already gotten approved. Here too there is a note of humor. Haman has worked to annihilate every Jew except the one that gets his goat.

It has been thought that at fifty cubits, or about eighty feet, the structure that Haman is advised to erect in 5:14 is too large to be a stake, which would come from a single tree, and must thus be a gallows instead.[159] This may be, but given the tendency of the book to gross exaggeration (e.g., the 127 provinces [1:1], the 180-day party [1:4], and the twelve months of cosmetic work [2:12]), such realism is out of order. That the action in question was to be performed on Haman's ten sons *after* they had been killed (9:6–10, 13) strongly argues for impalement on stakes rather than hanging on gallows. The point of impalement is not punishment, but exposure to disgrace.[160] Simply killing Mordecai would not assuage what feels like an enormous injury to Haman, with his fragile ego. Only an enormous, visible disgrace of Mordecai will bring him satisfaction.

VI. A Patriot Is Honored
and an Egomaniac Is Disgraced

Esther 6:1–14

6:1 That night sleep eluded the king, and he ordered the book of records, the annals, to be brought in, and they were read in the presence of the king. 2 Therein it was found recorded that Mordecai had informed on Bigthan[a] and Teresh, two of the king's eunuchs who guarded the thresh-

---

[158]See Talmon, " 'Wisdom,' " and Gerleman, 102.
[159]E.g., Paton, 240.
[160]Gerleman, 134.

old, who had sought to lay hands upon King Ahasuerus. 3 "What honor
or promotion has been conferred on Mordecai for this?" the king asked.
The king's courtiers who were in attendance upon him replied, "Nothing has been done for him." 4 "Who is in the court?" the king asked.
Haman was coming into the outer court of the royal palace to recommend
to the king that he have Mordecai impaled on the stake that he had prepared for him. 5 "Here is Haman standing in the court," the king's
courtiers replied, and the king said, "Let him enter." 6 When Haman had
entered, the king said to him, "What should be done for the man whom
the king desires to honor?" Said Haman to himself, "Whom would the
king desire to honor more than me?" 7 So Haman said to the king, "The
man whom the king desires to honor . . . 8 Let royal garb be brought that
the king has worn and a horse on which the king has ridden and on whose
head a royal diadem has been set.[b] 9 And let the garb and the horse be delivered into the care of one of the king's noble officials, and let the man
whom the king desires to honor be attired and led through the city square
mounted on the horse, while they call out before him: 'This is what is
done for the man whom the king desires to honor.'" 10 "Hurry, then!" the
king said to Haman. "Get the garb and the horse, as you have said, and
do so for Mordecai the Jew, who sits in the king's gate. Omit nothing of
all that you have said!" 11 So Haman got the garb and the horse, attired
Mordecai, led him mounted through the city square, and called out before him: "This is what is done for the man the king desires to honor."

12 Then Mordecai returned to the king's gate, whereas Haman hurried
home in mourning, with his head covered. 13 Then Haman told his wife
Zeresh and all his friends all that had happened to him. His advisers and
his wife Zeresh said to him, "If Mordecai, before whom you have begun
to fall, is of Jewish descent, you will never overcome him. You shall collapse altogether before him."

14 While they were still speaking with him, the king's eunuchs arrived
and rushed Haman to the banquet Esther had prepared.

a. Here, the name is *bigtānā'* as opposed to *bigtān* in 2:21. The variation is not significant.
b. The last clause does not appear in the LXX and raises semantic problems that are
discussed in the commentary.

Chapter 6 can be categorized equally well as farce and as omen. The farcical elements involve Haman's enormously foolish miscalculation as to the man
whom the king would wish to honor (vv. 4–9) and the ensuing ludicrous scene
in which the prime minister is compelled to serve as a herald for his archen-

emy, the lesser courtier, Mordecai the Jew (vv. 10–11). The ominous dimension becomes explicit in the words of Zeresh and Haman's friends in v. 13: The farce just enacted is only a foretaste of the inevitable triumph of the Jew over his enemy.

The chapter begins with the king's mysterious inability to sleep (v. 1). Some Jewish commentators have attributed Ahasuerus's insomnia to his nervousness about what Esther could possibly intend to request at the second banquet (5:8). Since she already has the highest status available to her, she must be planning to ask something for someone else, specifically for her foster father Mordecai. This in turn explains why the report of Mordecai's informing on the two assassins was found in the annals (v. 2): the king was looking for the grounds upon which Esther would base her request.[161] One serious problem with this is that it presupposes that Ahasuerus knows of Esther's relation to Mordecai and thus of her Jewishness, but there is no evidence to this effect. It is more likely that the king's insomnia is another one of those strangely unmotivated events, like Vashti's refusal to come to the banquet (1:12), Esther's winning the favor of all who see her (2:9, 15, 17; 5:2), and Mordecai's refusal to bow to Haman (3:2–4). Actions seem to come out of nowhere in this tale, but they gradually link together to form an immensely positive and meaningful pattern of Jewish deliverance: If the term "theology" means anything in reference to the book of Esther, this is its theology. That Ahasuerus could not sleep one night would be trivial, except for the coincidence that the records read to him as a soporific happen to be open to the report of Mordecai's unrequited benefaction. Similarly, that the king asks for advice as to how to repay his loyal courtier (6:3) would hardly be worth mentioning, except that Haman—in another strangely coincidental turn—happens to be entering the court at just that moment (v. 4): The timing could not be more perfect. The ground is thus laid for the minidrama of vv. 10–11, which is a foretaste in a comical, or even farcical, mode of the denouement of this entire intensely serious tale. The laugh that the reader has at Haman's expense here anticipates the joyous celebration of the Jews when he and his cohorts have been dispatched and, concurrently, when Mordecai and Esther have risen to commanding positions within the empire (chaps. 8–9).

Haman's insecurity and the egocentrism that it engenders are once again the source of his problem. He cannot imagine that the king could wish to honor anyone other than him (or "more than" him; the expression at the end of 6:6 is ambiguous). His eagerness to arrange public honors for himself stands in instructive contrast to Mordecai's reticence about his own valid claim to public honors—his saving of the king's life. This is the familiar contrast of the wise man who knows when to be silent and when to speak, choosing his words

---

[161]See, e.g., *Yosef Leqaḥ* to 6:1.

carefully, and the dullard who speaks too much and too soon, destroying himself in the process (cf., e.g., Prov. 12:19–28).

There are, nonetheless, some hints in the text that Haman's thinking of himself as "the man whom the king desires to honor" (Esth. 6:6) may not be so absurd as it first seems. In several parables in the Hebrew Bible, it is the addressee himself about whom the parable speaks. The key moment comes when the addressee is made to see this. Nathan's parable about the rich man who took the poor man's ewe (2 Sam. 12:1–12) is a particularly fine example. Its climax comes when Nathan decodes it to David: "That man is you!" (v. 7). Similarly, the wise woman of Tekoa's parable becomes intelligible to David only when he realizes that the woman has assumed his own role and her remaining son represents Absalom (2 Sam. 14:1–24, esp. v. 21;[162] cf. also Gen. 38:25–26). Part of the comedy of Esther 6 is that the expectations are reversed: the riddle is posed not *to* the king but *by* the king, and the answer to it is not the addressee, but his nemesis. Haman's attempt at cleverness proves his foolishness, just as his effort to come to court early in order to do in Mordecai (v. 4) results in his having to honor Mordecai (v. 11). As Moore puts it, "here the early bird is gotten by the worm."[163]

There may be another hint that the narrator has cleverly played a role of his own in snaring Haman to the benefit of Mordecai. When the king first learns that Mordecai's loyalty has gone unrewarded, he asks, "What honor (*yĕqār*) or promotion (*gĕdûllâ*) has been conferred on Mordecai for this?" (v. 3), but when he poses the same question to Haman, he leaves out not only Mordecai's name but also the second term and asks only, "What should be done for the man whom the king desires to honor (*yĕqār*)?" (v. 6). Had he again mentioned the promotion here, it could reasonably have been inferred that he was not speaking of Haman, whom he had already promoted (*giddal*) above all the other officials in the empire (3:1; 5:11).[164] By leaving out all specific mention of Mordecai (including his patriotic deed) and by speaking only of honor (which Haman craves) and not of high status (which he already has), the narrator (through the king) sets Haman up for the fall. But this succeeds only because of Haman's overweening pride and his gross overestimation of his own intelligence.

The syntax of Haman's answer to the king's question (in 6:7) recalls the syntax of Esther's answer in 5:7 ("The man whom the king desires to honor . . ." and "My wish and my request . . ."). The dangling phrase of 6:7 need not be the problem in Hebrew that it is in English, but the similarity with the exchange in the previous chapter is suggestive. It invites a contrast between Es-

[162]Bardtke, 347.

[163]Moore, *Esther,* 64.

[164]*Yosef Leqaḥ* to 6:6.

ther's circumspection and Haman's exhibitionism. She follows up with the conventional expression of deference ("If I have won Your Majesty's favor and if it please Your Majesty," 5:8), whereas he follows with a grandiose fantasy ("Let royal garb be brought . . . " 6:8). If 6:7 is truly an anacoluthon and is not to be construed with v. 8 as one sentence (as Hebrew syntax also allows), it conveys the impression that the delicious words "[t]he man whom the king desires to honor" are still echoing in Haman's head—his narcissism is momentarily preventing him from formulating an effective reply to the king's question.

The reply that he finally devises ought to have made the king raise his eyebrows (6:8–9). For Haman proposes that the royal honoree be dressed as the king himself and paraded through the town on one of the king's own horses. It is unclear whether the royal diadem to which Haman refers is to have been set upon the *horse's* head (as indicated in our translation, for which there is some grammatical and ethnological support[165]) or upon the *king's* head when he rode the horse in a ritual of enthronement.[166] If the latter is the case, then the closest analogy in the Hebrew Bible is to 1 Kings 1:33, in which David initiates Solomon's accession by having him ride upon the king's own mule.

The investiture in regal garb that Haman fantasizes has a number of parallels, the closest being Pharaoh's investiture and ritual parading of Joseph in Gen. 41:37–43. The contrast between these two texts, however, is as revealing as the similarity. Joseph is rewarded for devising a plan to save the kingdom during the coming seven lean years: the "man of discernment and wisdom" (Gen. 41:33) that he suggests Pharaoh appoint turns out to be himself. Haman has done nothing to merit a reward (a point that does not seem to have occurred to him). Rather, he seeks to displace "the man whom the king desires to honor"—the one who has, in fact, already saved the king's life. Joseph suggests a plan to benefit everyone and is rewarded with an investiture and a parade for himself. Haman suggests an investiture and a parade to benefit himself and is rewarded by having to hail his archenemy, the king's true benefactor. Note also that the king personally invests Joseph with the insignia of his office and assigns him "the chariot of the second-in-command" for the parade (Gen. 41:42–43). Haman, in contrast, does not specify who will invest him and requires that he ride on "a horse on which the king [himself] has ridden" (Esth. 6:8). The subordination of the honoree to the monarch is much clearer in the case of Joseph than in Haman's case. Indeed, if the analogy with David and Solomon in 1 Kings 1:33 is added into the mix, one might just suspect that Haman aspires to succeed the king and not simply to be honored for having served him well. As things turn out (Esth. 6:10–11), by reaching too high, he

---

[165]See Ibn Ezra to 6:8.
[166]See Gerleman, 117–18.

has brought himself low: It is Mordecai who will play Joseph's role of second-in-command, attired in majestic garb (8:15; 10:3; cf. esp. Gen. 41:45b).

The investiture in royal garb that Haman seeks for himself and that Mordecai actually receives is reminiscent of the ancient Mesopotamian institution of the substitute king, of which echoes were still heard in the time of Xerxes.[167] The problem is that the substitute king was essentially a scapegoat, dying in place of the real king, whereas Haman seeks the role of king but meets his demise, and Mordecai goes on to glory. Perhaps these reversals of our expectations constitute yet another instance of the storyteller's humor and satirizing of the great imperial court.

It is here in chap. 6 that we have our first premonition that Haman will receive retribution according to the principle of measure for measure that figures so importantly in biblical morality (e.g., Lev. 24:19; Deut. 19:19; 1 Sam. 15:33; Obad. 15). His serving as a herald of Mordecai in Esth. 6:11 is an obvious adumbration of his coming fall and the concurrent rise of Mordecai in his stead (7:5–8:2, 15–17), as Zeresh and his advisers point out to him (v. 13). But chap. 6 also reverses certain previous injustices along the same retributive principle. Moore astutely observes that "just as Haman had managed in iii 8 to conceal from the king the identity of 'a certain people,' so here the king unintentionally . . . keeps from Haman the identity of Mordecai as 'the man whom the king especially wants to honor.'"[168] In addition, note the identical words, "all that had happened to him" (*'ēt kol-'ăšer qārāhû*) in 6:13, in which Haman tells Zeresh and his friends about his public disgrace, and in 4:7, in which Mordecai informs Esther of the plan to annihilate the Jews.[169] The implication would seem to be that the second set of events has begun the seemingly impossible task of reversing the first. It may be that Haman's hurrying (*nidḥap*) home in disgrace (6:12) is to be seen as the first sign of the reversal of the decree of genocide that the couriers relayed posthaste (*dĕḥûpîm*, 3:15). Note also that now it is Haman who is "in mourning" and Mordecai who is dressed in royal fashion, quite the opposite of where things stood in chap. 4 (cf. 4:1 and 6:12). The situation is looking up for the Jews.

It is unclear how Haman's wife Zeresh and his advisers know that if Mordecai is of Jewish stock, Haman can never overcome him but must fall before him (6:13). It is possible that the advisers (*ḥăkāmîm*) are cast in the same mold as those in 1:13, "the sages (*ḥăkāmîm*) learned in precedents," and have astrology in their repertory of skills. If this is the case, then they interpret the minidrama of chap. 6 as an omen of things to come. The words, "[i]f Mordecai . . . is of Jewish descent," however, suggest an alternative: Haman's advis-

---

[167]See n. 1, above.
[168]Moore, *Esther*, 67.
[169]Hakham, 43.

ers and his wife, knowing of the scriptural predictions of Israel's triumph (e.g., Num. 24:15–19) and Amalek's demise (e.g., Num. 24:20), interpret Haman's humiliation as the first stage in the fulfillment of these prophecies in their own time[170] (on Haman as an Amalekite, see the commentary on Esth. 2:5 and 3:1). Perhaps the word *zera'* ("descent") plays a role here, for it is Abraham's *zera'* (in the sense of progeny) to whom the LORD gives an indefeasable promise of national greatness (e.g., Gen. 13:15–16). The LXX adds the words "for the living God is with him" at the end of 6:13. The theology of the surviving Hebrew text of Esther is more circumspect and more subtle. The MT of this verse hints at some uncanny force ensuring the triumph of the Jews, as in 4:14, but, as was the case there, it does not identify the mysterious source of the deliverance of the Jews and the downfall of their foes. One can also compare Judith 5:17, in which Achior the Ammonite tells the Assyrian commander Holofernes that the Jews are invincible so long as they do not sin, since the LORD protects them.

No sooner has Haman received the bad news concerning Mordecai's invincibility than he is hurried off to the climactic banquet with Ahasuerus and Esther (6:14). Whereas the last time Zeresh and Haman's friends spoke to him, they advised him to impale Mordecai and then to go to the king's banquet joyfully (5:14), now Haman is doubtless in a very different mood. He is marching to his own destruction.

VII. The Climactic Banquet

Esther 7:1–10

7:1 So the king and Haman came to the banquet that Esther had prepared. 2 Again on that second day, during the wine-drinking, the king said to Esther, "What is your wish, Queen Esther? It shall be granted to you! What is your request? Up to half the empire—it shall be fulfilled!" 3 Queen Esther answered, saying, "If I have won Your favor, O King, and if it please Your Majesty, let my life be granted me as my wish, and my people as my request. 4 For we have been sold—I and my people— to be destroyed, slain, and annihilated. Had we been sold only into slavery, men and women alike, I would have kept my silence, for then the adversary would not have been worth the king's loss."[a] 5 King Ahasuerus said, speaking to Queen Esther, "Who is the guy and where is the guy who has had the nerve to do this?"[b] 6 "An adversary and an enemy," said Esther, "—this evil fellow Haman." Haman was stricken with terror

---

[170]Paton, 256.

before the king and queen. 7 The king got up in a rage and left the wine-drinking for the courtyard, while Haman stayed to plead with Queen Esther for his life, for he saw that the king's animus against him was absolute. 8 When the king returned from the courtyard to the drinking-hall, Haman was falling onto the couch upon which Esther reclined. "Does he also intend," said the king, "to violate the queen while I am in the palace?" No sooner did these words leave the king's mouth than Haman's face blanched.ᶜ 9 Then Harbona, one of the eunuchs in attendance upon the king, said, "Not only that, but at Haman's house a stake fifty cubits high is standing that Haman made for Mordecai—who spoke in support of the king." "Impale him on it!" the king commanded. 10 So Haman was impaled on the stake that he had set up for Mordecai, and the king's rage abated.

a. The last clause is problematic. The word *ṣār* can mean either "adversary" (as in Zech. 8:10) or "adversity" (as in Ps. 4:2). The use of the word *nēzeq,* which usually denotes a financial loss, may suggest "adversity" rather than "adversary," as many scholars have thought. But Ahasuerus's question about who is behind this in v. 5 suggests that Esther's plaintive speech included reference to an individual, and this turns out to be "[a]n adversary [*ṣār*] and an enemy," Haman (v. 6), elsewhere known as "the enemy (*ṣōrēr*) of the Jews" (3:10; 8:1; 9:10, 24). So interpreted, the clause means that Esther would not bring the king's prime minister down merely to cancel a sale of her people into slavery, but annihilation is another matter and supersedes any financial loss the king may sustain by counteracting his previous decree.

b. "[G]uy" has been chosen to convey the derogatory connotation of *zeh* here.

c. The last word (*ḥāpû*) probably means "they covered" and is thus often taken to refer to a ceremony of disgrace directed at a criminal or a person otherwise out of favor. Though there is some evidence for the practice in the Greco-Roman world,[171] it is unattested in ancient Persia or Israel. Moreover, if we are to read the clause as "they covered Haman's face," the word order is unusual. The simplest solution is to assume the loss of one letter (*r*) and read *ḥāpĕrû,* "blanched," which is plural to agree with *pĕnê,* "face" (cf. Ps. 34:6).

The brevity of v. 1 (just seven words in Hebrew) reinforces the impression conveyed by the image of the king's eunuchs' "rushing" Haman to the second banquet (6:14); the matter is hurrying to a climax. As in the case of the first banquet, the king gets down to business immediately, asking, now for the third time, "What is your wish, Queen Esther? It shall be granted to you! What is your request? Up to half the empire—it shall be fulfilled!" (7:2; cf. 5:3, 6). There are some interesting variations in the phrasing among the three occurrences. In the first (5:3), which comes during the highly charged scene of Esther's approaching the king unbidden, we find the shortest version. "What is

171See, e.g., Paton, 264.

bothering you?" there takes the place of half of the parallelistic utterance, thus underscoring the irregular nature of Esther's approach and perhaps the king's favorable disposition as well. The title "Queen Esther," which appears there and here (but not in 5:6), may also serve to underscore the king's favor in these two enormously suspenseful scenes. More intriguing is the gender of the verb "it shall be granted," which is masculine in the first two occurrences (*yinnātēn,* 5:3, 6), but feminine in the climactic third position (*tinnātēn,* 7:2).[172] This change helps signal that this time Queen Esther will ask for something different, something vastly more important, it turns out, than just another banquet. The femininity of the verb anticipates the feminine predicate of her reply in the next verse (v. 3) dictated by the key word, "my life" (*napšî,* a feminine noun). This time Esther asks not for a banquet (*mišteh,* a masculine noun), as before, but for her very survival.

Her plea is masterfully constructed. Note that she addresses the king first not in the expected third-person form ("If I have won the King's favor. . . ."; cf. 5:4, 8) but in the bolder and more personal form of direct address ("If I have won Your favor, O King . . . ," v. 3). She is pleading for her own life but also implying, without being so tactless as to say it directly, that the king is about to lose the person dearest to him and most intimate with him. Just as Memucan's plan deprived Ahasuerus of Queen Vashti (1:16–20; cf. 1:19 and 7:3), so will following Haman's more nefarious plan deprive the king of someone more precious to him, Queen Esther herself. It is her personal favor in the eyes of the king that moves him to countermand the death sentence upon her entire people.

There is a close parallel to this in Exodus 33, in which Moses pleads with the LORD to renege on his declaration that he will not personally accompany Israel into the promised land after the catastrophe of the golden calf. Time and again Moses refers to his own personal favor in the eyes of the LORD (vv. 12 and 13 [twice]). The LORD then relents somewhat, but employs the second-person singular, not the plural (v. 14), implying that only Moses himself and not the entire people will benefit. To this Moses retorts, "How will it be known, therefore, that I have found favor in Your eyes—I and Your people—unless You go with us, so that we may be distinguished—I and Your people—from every other people on the face of the earth?" (v. 16). This works. "Even this thing that you have asked, I will do," the LORD says, "because you have found favor in my eyes" (v. 17). Like Esther, Moses is the sovereign's darling, and like her, he pleads not simply for himself but for his people, boldly risking the favor that he has won in hopes of having it extended to the entire nation of Israel. And in each case the gamble succeeds.

Esther 7:4 picks up the language of the king's original genocidal edict—"to destroy, slay, and annihilate" (3:13). Whether Esther's statement that she and

---

[172]See *Yosef Leqaḥ* to 7:2.

her people have been "sold" (*mkr*) is to be taken literally is a matter of some uncertainty. As we saw in our discussion of 3:11, it is unclear whether the king finally accepted Haman's offer of 10,000 silver talents. It should be noticed that in some other biblical texts *mkr* means "to hand over" (especially to destruction) rather than "to sell" (e.g., Deut. 32:30; Judg. 4:9), and Esth. 7:4 may be another case of this.[173] The same verse can, however, be interpreted to support the notion that the Jews had indeed been sold. In this case, Esther reminds Ahasuerus of the information she learned from Mordecai in 4:7, "the story of the money that Haman had offered to deposit in the royal treasury in exchange for the destruction of the Jews." In further support of the letter interpretation, one can cite Neh. 5:8, in which Nehemiah reports having taken action to buy back Jews who were "sold" (*mkr*) to Gentiles. Given Nehemiah's origin as a Jewish official in the court of the Persian emperor in the fortified compound of Susa (Neh. 1:1–2, 11b), the relevance of this verse is heightened.

The order of the words "I and my people" in Esth. 7:4 may seem selfish, but only if one loses sight of Esther's rhetorical strategy and the parallel in Exod. 33:16. The queen appeals first to Ahasuerus's affection (or lust) for her. Only if this approach succeeds can she expand his range of awareness to include her whole threatened race. Afterward, she moves on to an appeal to the king's pride. The king is too important to bother with a mere sale of innocent people (including herself) into slavery, she tells him; it is their destruction, slaughter, and annihilation that has brought her to petition in her own and their behalf. As one scholar puts it:

> It is the implied suggestion that he would be willing to dishonor her for money which challenges his honor. . . . But it is because her honor is respectfully placed in his hands that *he* must maintain it. Certainly it would be a disgraceful thing for *him* if she were sold off into slavery."[174]

But one should not miss the humor in the implication that the king and his interests are so important that the queen would prefer to be sold into slavery (along with her entire people) rather than to bring such a paltry matter to his attention. This is, after all, the same queen who has already taken her life into her hands to solicit the king on behalf of her people (Esth. 4:15–5:5). Esther's pose as a weak and helpless woman who must rely on her husband may have fooled him (fool that he is), but the joke is on him, not on the reader.

The repetition of the word *wayyō'mer,* rendered above as "said, saying," in Esth. 7:5 is perplexing and perhaps owing to scribal error. If it is authentic, it may perhaps indicate the degree of the king's upset: he is so angry that he can

[173]Ibid., on 7:4.

[174]Timothy Laniak, "The Scroll of Esther: A Tale of Honor and Shame," seminar paper, Harvard University, 1994, 18.

only sputter.[175] The odd structure of his actual words ("Who is the guy and where is the guy . . . ?") adds plausibility to this surmise. If we assume that 7:4 is Esther's first disclosure of her Jewishness, then we can imagine why the king is reduced nearly to incoherence. Esther's plea in 7:4, however, never specified who her endangered people were, just as Haman's proposal of genocide in 3:8 never named the "certain people" whom the king should annihilate.[176] This makes it possible that Ahasuerus has known of Esther's Jewishness for some time, but has not realized—or has not remembered—that it was the Jewish nation whose destruction he had authorized. In its demand to know "who had the nerve (*mělā'ô libbô*) to do this" (7:5), Ahasuerus's question is similarly open to multiple interpretations, none of them flattering to the king. He may be simply trying to disavow responsibility, as Esther's plea in the previous verse allows, since it seems to assume that he does not know that she is endangered by the genocidal project. Or it may be that he knows that he has authorized some group's destruction but is irate that the person proposing the project had, without telling the king, targeted the group that includes his beloved queen. Lastly, he may be so angry or so confused (perhaps from inebriation) that the whole plan to perpetrate genocide has slipped his mind.

Couched as two sets of three words in Hebrew ("an-adversarial [man] and-an-enemy, this evil-fellow Haman"), Esther's reply (7:6) parallels the structure of Ahasuerus's question in the previous verse ("Who is the-guy, and where is the-guy?"),[177] just as her reply in 7:3 ("let my life be granted me as my wish, and my people as my request") mirrors his question in the verse before ("What is your wish? . . . What is your request?"). This gives the sense of a couple dancing beautifully together, but only because the woman is able to absorb the man's jerky motions with the utmost grace and poise, or, to change the metaphor, it reminds one of two tennis players nicely matched, but only because one of them proves able to return the other's uncontrolled volleys in a way that is supremely effective but in no way aggressive or hostile. When Haman is "stricken with terror before the king and queen" (7:6), we have a dramatic enactment of the psychological reality that Esther has brilliantly engineered. Haman has been split off from Ahasuerus, and the king and the queen now stand together against the man who has been labeled as their common enemy, not "the enemy of the Jews" (*ṣōrēr hayyěhûdîm*), as is usually the case (3:10; 8:1; 9:10, 24), but rather "an enemy and an adversary" in general (*'îš ṣar wě'ôyēb*). It is no longer the Persians against the Jews, but the Persians and the Jews against the anti-Semites.

Why the king stomps out in a huff (Esth. 7:7) has been the subject of much

---

[175]Ibn Ezra to 7:5.

[176]Note also the common use of the odd expression *'ên šōweh* in these two verses.

[177]Roberta Stong, " 'My petition and my request': An Analysis of Esther 5:1–8 and 7:1–6," seminar paper, Harvard University, 1994, 13.

speculation, summarized nicely by Paton.[178] Perhaps, for example, he wants "to avoid sight of the hated Haman" or "to think about his decision." Perhaps "he was still friendly to Haman and hesitated to condemn him," or, on the other hand, "uncomfortably heated with wine and anger." Whatever the reason, the image of Ahasuerus, lord over 127 provinces from India to Ethiopia, absenting himself just at the climactic moment is a comic touch that reinforces our sense of him as weak, malleable, and devoid of self-control (see the commentary on chap. 1). The "rage" associated with his precipitous departure in 7:7 appears as a familiar trait of his character, having been mentioned twice before, both times in connection with Vashti's insubordination (1:12; 2:1). It is a trait that he shares with Haman, who has also been described twice as filled with "rage," both times in connection with another act of insubordination, Mordecai's (3:5; 5:9). Esther 7:7 thus serves to remind us of Ahasuerus and Haman's similarity, while at the same time telling of their separation and of the king's total animosity toward his prime minister. We can go further: With Esther's revelation of the name of her people's mortal enemy in 7:6, it is now Haman who is being categorized as insubordinate, so that the object of the third mention of the king's rage is thus no longer Vashti, who is long gone, but Haman, who is about to be dispatched.

Chapter 7, verse 8 presents us with perhaps the funniest scene in the whole book of Esther. By having Ahasuerus stomp out in the previous verse, the author allows him to misperceive the intention behind Haman's falling onto Esther's couch when he returns. Falling down before a superior is a familiar gesture of supplication in the Hebrew Bible (e.g., 8:3; 1 Sam. 25:24), but Ahasuerus mistakes Haman's action for a sexual assault. Haman, for his part, must think that since all the authorities have on him so far is conspiracy to commit genocide, there is still hope for pardon. In light of Ahasuerus's character, the hope may not have been altogether unrealistic. It is dashed, however, when Ahasuerus catches Haman attempting something that in his moral calculus is vastly worse—making a move on his woman. When the king so interprets his prime minister's gesture, the voluble Haman is, seemingly miraculously, rendered speechless: The end draws nigh.

That an act of falling (*npl*) seals Haman's fate (7:8) is pregnant with meaning and refulgent with the reflections of previous verses in the book. It was, for example, Mordecai's refusal to prostrate himself before the new prime minister that evoked the latter's anti-Jewish plan (3:1–6) and that has now ultimately forced Haman to prostrate himself before a Jewess. The first move in that plan was Haman's causing the lot to be cast (*npl*) before him (3:7). Then when, in a foreshadowing of his final demise, Haman is forced to run before Mordecai, hailing him as "the man whom the king desires to honor" (6:11), his advisers and his

[178]Paton, 262.

wife tell him that "[i]f Mordecai, before whom you have begun to fall (*npl*), is of Jewish descent, you will never overcome him. You shall collapse altogether (*npl*, twice) before him" (6:13). Given the presence of a number of verbs that are used in the Hebrew Bible to refer to a person's ruin, the use of *npl* in 6:13 is all the more ominous in the light of Haman's misinterpreted gesture in 7:8.

But with the king in an even greater rage because of Haman's perceived sexual assault upon the queen, he is still unable to formulate a coherent response until one of his eunuchs, Harbona, suggests the obvious answer of impaling the conspirator upon the stake he has erected for Mordecai, the king's personal savior (7:9). It is as though Ahasuerus, even after all that has happened, is still unable to tell the villains from the heroes without prompting. That it is Harbona, a relatively lowly figure, not one of the king's seven official sages (see 1:10, 13–14) who provides him the prompting is yet another comic inversion: The lowborn tells the highborn what to do (though in a way that wisely allows the king himself to utter the actual imperative: "Impale him on it!"). Haman's being hoist with his own petard conforms to a more general biblical pattern in which the punishment reflects the crime (e.g., Exod. 22:21–23; Lev. 24:19; Deut. 19:16–19; 1 Sam. 15:23b, 33). Here, however, there is no mention of divine causation. It is Harbona and Ahasuerus, not God, who bring about the condign punishment. In this, Esther may show the influence of wisdom literature, which sometimes speaks of an inherent correspondence of deed and consequence, even apart from divine intervention (e.g., Prov. 26:27).[179]

With Haman's impalement, the king's rage once again abates (Esth. 7:10), just as his rage against Vashti abated after he issued his royal decree forbidding her to approach him and ordering all women to treat their husbands with honor (2:1). It is another indication both of Ahasuerus's volatility and of the homology of Haman to Vashti. It nicely prepares us for the central inversions in the next chapter, when Mordecai succeeds Haman just as Esther had succeeded Vashti (8:15–17).

Though some commentators have faulted Esther for not responding positively to Haman's abject supplications in 7:7, Moore's retort is closer to the mark and warrants a full citation:

> The simple truth is that at this point Haman was not defeated: he was a falling, not a fallen enemy. He had lost a crucial battle, but he had not necessarily lost the war. Were Haman to survive this round, he might recover and score a knockout in the next. So long as an enemy as powerful and shrewd as Haman lived, he was a threat to Esther, Mordecai, and the Jewish community. To say here that Esther was merciless and unfeeling is to misinterpret the entire situation. Thus, while her heart might have prompted her to be merciful, logic and prudence restrained her.[180]

---

[179]See Talmon, " 'Wisdom.' "
[180]Moore, *Esther,* 74.

One might add that given Haman's Amalekite associations and their resonance
in the biblical symbolic order (see the commentary on 2:5 and 3:1), a true
change of heart on his part is out of the question, and Esther would be irre-
sponsible if she stood between him and his just doom. More fundamentally,
though the tradition of giving the book of Esther a moralistic reading is of great
antiquity, one can wonder whether a narrative so full of intrigue, comedy, and
farce should be interpreted with such high seriousness. To demand that Esther
herself be a paragon of morality for ordinary people may be grossly to misun-
derstand the genre of the book itself and to miss the special circumstances of
the episode it claims to report.

VIII. Esther's Renewed Plea Brings Results

Esther 8:1–17

1. The Queen Persuades Ahasuerus to Act (8:1–8)

8:1 On that same day, King Ahasuerus gave the estate of Haman, enemy of the Jews, to Queen Esther, and Mordecai came into the king's
presence, for Esther had disclosed his relationship to her. 2 The king
took off his signet ring, which he had taken away from Haman, and
gave it to Mordecai, and Esther put Mordecai in charge of Haman's estate. 3 Esther again spoke before the king. Falling at his feet and crying, she begged him to avert the calamity that Haman the Agagite had
plotted against the Jews. 4 When the king extended the golden scepter
to Esther, she got up, stood before the king, 5 and said, "If it please
Your Majesty and if I have won Your favor, and if the proposal seems
appropriate to Your Majesty and I am pleasing in Your estimation, let
an order be drawn up to withdraw the letters that Haman son of
Hammedatha wrote in connection with his plot to annihilate the Jews
in all the king's provinces. 6 For how can I bear to behold the ruin that
will befall my people, and how can I bear to behold the annihilation of
my family?"

7 Then King Ahasuerus said to Queen Esther and to Mordecai the Jew,
"I have given Haman's estate to Esther, and he has been impaled upon a
stake because he threatened to lay hands upon the Jews. 8 But you, draw
up a writ concerning the Jews as you see fit. Do so in the king's name

and seal it with the king's signet ring. For a writ drawn up in the king's name and sealed with the king's signet ring cannot be withdrawn."

Esther 8:1 introduces the theme of the enormous reversal that has taken place, a theme that will occupy the rest of chap. 8 and chap. 9 as well. When "[o]n that same day" King Ahasuerus awards Haman's estate to Queen Esther, he not only follows the Persian practice of state confiscation of a convicted criminal's property;[181] he also reverses Esth. 3:9, in which Haman offered the king a bribe to accept his plan to annihilate the Jews: now the king takes the wealth *from* Haman and gives it *to* the savior of the Jews. This act "[o]n that same day" is also a dramatic reversal of Haman's plan to kill and despoil the Jews "on a single day" (Esth. 3:13). Similarly, Esther's disclosure of her relationship to Mordecai reverses her cousin's earlier prohibition upon revealing her people and her family (2:10, 20). And Mordecai's coming into the king's presence "on that same day" reverses Haman's approach on "[t]hat night" with the hope of securing the king's approval to impale his nemesis, the insubordinate Jew Mordecai (6:1–5). The king's transfer of his signet ring from Haman to Mordecai (8:2a), which must have taken place before Haman's impalement in 7:10, reverses the king's gesture in 3:10, by which he signified his acceptance of the plan to rid the kingdom of Jews. Finally, Esther's placing Mordecai over Haman's estate (8:2b) realizes the prediction of the late prime minister's advisers and his wife that he shall never overcome the Jew but shall collapse before him (6:13). Mordecai's dominance over Haman, pre-enacted in the farcical parade of 6:11, has now been finalized and solemnized.

From the similarity of Esth. 8:4 to 5:1–2, it appears that Esther is once again risking her life by initiating conversation with the king. Her resumption of speech in 8:3 seems to be based on a point that the dramatic reversals of vv. 1–2 have subtly obscured: Ahasuerus has granted her things for which she has not asked—Haman's estate and Mordecai's promotion—but he has neglected or tacitly refused to grant what she wanted most, the deliverance of the Jews from their death sentence (7:3–4).[182] This augments our impression of the king as lacking all sense of proportion and priority. His dealing with property while matters of life itself hang in the balance suggests that the scene in which Haman bribes him (or offers to) in order to destroy the Jews (3:8–11) has not been altogether overturned after all. The king hands Haman's estate over to Esther, yet the latter's life and that of all her nation remain in direct peril because of the king's own unacknowledged decree. The verb *npl* ("[f]alling") in 8:3 reinforces this sense of unfinished business. Here this important word (see the commentary on 7:8) has the same meaning it had in 7:8, when Haman fell in

---

[181]Herodotus 3:129; Josephus, *Ant.* 11:17.
[182]*Yosef Leqaḥ* to 8:3.

supplication upon Esther's couch, unwittingly ensuring that this gesture, mistaken for a sexual assault, would have the inverse effect. Now it is Esther who falls before Ahasuerus to beg that he "avert (*he'ĕbîr*) the calamity that Haman the Agagite had plotted against the Jews," just as he had "taken away" (*he'ĕbîr*) the signet ring from Haman and given it to Mordecai (8:2). The problem here is that with the same root (*'br*) the author has already told us that a law of the Persians and Medes cannot be "revoked."[183]

Perhaps that is why Esther pulls out all the stops in her effort to persuade the king to withdraw the letters that Haman had written (8:5). Verse 5 is most reminiscent of 7:3, except that here Esther pleads only for her people and not, as there, for herself as well (and first). Note that the order of the clauses has also been reversed ("If it please Your Majesty and if I have won Your favor" in 8:5 versus "If I have won Your favor, O King, and it if please Your Majesty" in 7:3). In fact, the structure of 8:5a exhibits a highly rhythmic and parallelistic alternation of statements of the king's interest with Esther's personal attractiveness to him:[184]

A	If it please Your Majesty
B	and if I have won Your favor,
A'	and if the proposal seems appropriate to Your Majesty
B'	and I am pleasing in Your estimation

In her request itself, she cagily omits all reference to the king's role in issuing the lethal edict: she mentions only "the letters that Haman son of Hammedatha wrote" (8:5b).[185] Esther's plaintive reference to her "people" and her "family" (v. 6) again recalls Mordecai's prohibition upon her disclosing "her people and her family" (2:10; cf. 2:20, again in reverse order). Now that she has at last proven able to break her strategic silence, she invokes the suffering that her people's destruction will inflict upon her, in support of her extraordinary request that the genocidal edict be withdrawn. The Jews may mean nothing to King Ahasuerus, even after Mordecai has saved his life—so obtuse and morally insensate is he. But Esther means everything to him, and if their destruction causes her pain, perhaps it might still be prevented.

In 8:7, the king, striking an official tone, reviews his prior actions in the matter, which involve only the person of Haman and like Esther's petition omit all reference to his own role in authorizing the plot against the Jews. The words "lay hands upon the Jews" recall the conspiracy of the two eunuchs "to lay

---

[183]Fox, *Character*, 92.
[184]See *Yosef Leqaḥ* to 8:5.
[185]Bardtke, 365.

hands upon King Ahasuerus" (2:21) and thus very subtly associate Haman with insurrection and the Jews with the person of the king (cf. 3:6). This is exquisitely ironic, for it was their failure to submit to the king's laws that was the substance of Haman's accusation against the Jews (3:8). The link between the two conspiracies is, of course, Mordecai, who informs on the two eunuchs and dispatches Esther to plead on behalf of her people. If the last sentence in 8:8 is part of the king's speech rather than the narrator's explanation, as some have held,[186] then Ahasuerus is here telling Esther that even he cannot do what she asked and withdraw the first set of documents (cf. *lĕhāšîb* in v. 5 and *'ên lĕhāšîb* in v. 8). He can award her half the empire (5:3, 6; 7:2), but he, sovereign of the known world, cannot revoke his own decree. We have again the impression of a man entangled in his own state apparatus, the victim of his own regime, a prisoner of the legal order over which he presides. What he can do, however, is to promulgate a countervailing decree, and even the wording suggests that Haman's decree is now being opposed by Esther and Mordecai's. Note "as you see fit" in 8:8 and 3:11, indicating that in both instances the king is rather detached, always preferring to delegate even matters of life and death to his underlings.

2. A New Edict Is Issued (8:9–12)

8:9 And so, the king's scribes were summoned at that time, in the third month (that is, the month of Sivan), on its twenty-third day, and in accordance with all that Mordecai directed, a writ was drawn up and issued to the Jews and to the satraps, the governors, and the officials of the provinces from India to Ethiopia, one hundred twenty-seven provinces, to each province in its own script and to each people in its own language, and to the Jews in their own script and in their own language. **10** It was drawn up in the name of King Ahasuerus and sealed with the king's signet ring. Letters were dispatched by couriers riding swift horses, royal coursers bred from elite studs,[a] **11** to this effect: the king was granting the Jews in every city the right to assemble and to fight for their lives—to destroy, slay, and annihilate the armed forces of any people or province that might attack them, women and children as well, and to take their property as plunder, **12** throughout all of King Ahasuerus's provinces on a single day, the thirteenth day of the twelfth month (that is, the month of Adar).

a. The precise meaning of the equine terminology is unclear. *Rekeš,* here rendered as "swift horses," appears only in 8:14, in 1 Kings 5:8, and in Micah 1:13. *'Ăhaštĕrānîm,* a hapax legomenon, is usually and plausibly associated with a Persian

---

[186]E.g., Moore, *Esther,* 79.

word for "kingdom"—hence, "royal coursers." The last expression, *běnê hārammākîm,* combines the Hebrew word for "sons of" with another hapax legomenon, which seems to be the plural of a Hebrew noun in the formation of a *nomen agentis,* preceded by the definite article. The term has sometimes been associated with a Syriac word for "herdsman," but this provides scant illumination, and the ancient versions are as puzzled by the equine terminology as are the modern commentators and perhaps even the earliest readers and hearers of the book of Esther. The unfamiliar terminology suggests exotic animals associated with royalty.

Esther 8:9–12 is a reversal of 3:12–15, the report of the genocidal edict that Haman issued on the authority of King Ahasuerus.[187] Whereas those events took place on the thirteenth day of the first month (Nisan), these are dated to the twenty-third of the third month, Sivan, in early summer. All the intervening action thus occupied two months and ten days, perhaps suggesting a connection with the symbolic number seventy (e.g., cf. Gen. 46:27; Judg. 9:2, 4; Jer. 29:10; Ps. 90:10). Esther 8:9–12 resumes the lofty, officialistic tone with which the tale opened (cf. 1:1–9). Though it is conceivable that the double appearance of the phrase "to the Jews" in 8:9 is owing to scribal error, it is more probable that the author wishes to underscore the new safety involved in having a Jewish identity. After all, Mordecai, as the leader of the Jews (10:3), is now able to address his brothers directly and "in their own script and in their own language" to boot. Things have come very far from the time a short while ago when to be Jewish meant to be a vulnerable refugee (2:5–6, 10, 20). Now, as Fox remarks, "[t]he Jews' language is thus given official status."[188] In the corresponding account of Haman's edict, there is no special mention of the Jews' script and language (3:12) nor of the "swift horses, royal coursers bred from elite studs" (8:10; cf. 3:13). These special horses may be intended to highlight the better pedigree of the countervailing edict, which originates not with the Agagite prime minister but with the Jewish queen. Note that the first time a royal horse was mentioned, it was the king's own, ridden by Mordecai in his triumphal parade (6:8, 10–11). Perhaps we are to understand that the second set of horses was faster and thus a reflection of the king's anxiety to counteract the earlier missives. If so, there may be a comic touch here as well, since the day of the coming assaults against the Jews is still almost nine months off.

The substance of the new edict is that the Jews are now permitted to gather in self-defense, to slay the women and children of any that attack them, and to take booty (8:11). This closely mirrors the substance of the first edict (3:13). The killing of women and children, offensive to any decent moral sensibility today, is dictated by the symmetry of the two decrees, which in turn heightens

---

[187]See the helpful charts in Fox, *Character,* 102, and Craig, *Reading Esther,* 86–87.
[188]Fox, *Character,* 230.

the expectations of the day of decision. It is probably also colored by old cultic conceptions of combat. Note, for example, that Mordecai's kinsman Saul was commanded to kill the women and children of the Amalekites under the rule of Haman's kinsman Agag (1 Sam. 15:3; see the commentary on 2:5 and on 3:1). Note that in the actual event, the Jews of Mordecai's day decline to take spoil (9:10, 16).

The notion that people will refrain from acting in self-defense unless they have royal permission may be another comic element. But it may also be the case that the key words are "the right to assemble" (8:11): The new rescript grants the Jews permission to gather into military units on or before the day of hostilities.

The Text of the Edict

Chapter E:1–24 (= Esther 16:1–24 in the Vulgate)

E:1 *The following is a copy of the letter:*

The great king Artaxerxes to the governors of the provinces in the one hundred twenty-seven satrapies and to those who look after our interests: Greetings!

2 Having been honored through the enormous generosity of their benefactors, many have become more arrogant. 3 Not only do they seek to harm our subjects; unable to bear such bounty, they even attempt to scheme against their own benefactors. 4 Not only do they deprive people of gratitude, but, excited by the boasts of those deprived of all that is good, they assume that they will escape the evil-hating judgment of the God who always sees everything. 5 Often, too, the encouragement of friends entrusted with the management of affairs has made many of those placed in positions of authority accessories to the shedding of innocent blood and has involved them in irreparable misfortune 6 by deceiving the unmixed good will of those in power with false and malicious reasoning.

*7 This can be observed, not so much in the ancient stories that have been handed down, as by an examination of the wicked things wrought by the pestilence of those unworthy of exercising authority. 8 We must take action that will render the empire undisturbed and peaceful for all people, 9 taking advantage of changing situations*ª *and always deciding the matters that come into our purview equitably. 10 For example, Haman, the son of Hammedatha, a Macedonian, a man surely without Persian blood* *and quite different from us in goodness of heart, was received by us as a guest.* 11 *He so enjoyed the benevolence that we show to every nation that he was publicly proclaimed "father of the king" before whom all bow down as the person second to the royal throne.* 12 *Unable to contain his arrogance, he sought to deprive us of kingdom and of life.* 13 *Through intricate deceptions, he sought the annihilation of our savior and constant benefactor, Mordecai, and our blameless royal partner Esther, along with their entire race.* 14 *In this manner, he thought he would catch us helpless and transfer the hegemony of the Persians to the Macedonians.*

15 *We, however, find that the Jews, who were consigned to destruction by this arch-criminal, are not evildoers, but are governed by very just laws,* 16 *for they are the children of the Most High, the living God, who has maintained the empire for us and our forebears in the most beautiful order.*

17 *You will do well, therefore, not to act upon the letters sent by Haman, the son of Hammedatha,* 18 *inasmuch as the person who devised these things has been impaled with all his household before the gates of Susa — a most appropriate sentence promptly passed upon him by the God who rules over everything.*

19 *You shall post a copy of this letter publicly in every place in order to allow the Jews to practice their own customs* 20 *and to give them assistance so that they may defend themselves in the moment of their affliction, on that very day, the thirteenth of the twelfth month, Adar.* 21 *For God the omnipotent has turned it from the day of the destruction of the chosen people into one of joy for them.* 22 *Therefore, observe it among your commemorative festivals joyously as a special day,* 23 *so that both presently and in the future it may symbolize deliverance for you and well-disposed Persians and serve as a reminder of destruction to those who plot against you.* 24 *Any city or province whatsoever that does not act according to these orders shall be ruthlessly devastated by sword and fire. Not only shall it become untrodden by human beings, but it shall also become hateful to beasts and birds for all time.*

a. Some Greek manuscripts preface the word *ou* here, making the participle negative, a reading reflected also in the OL. If that reading is adopted, the point is that Artaxerxes will be more steadfast and less distractable in the future.

Chapter E, the fifth of the Greek additions to Esther, is best conceived as the counterpoint to chap. B. Whereas the latter purported to be the text of Artaxerxes's decree in support of Haman's plot against the Jews, this is the same king's rescript in support of Esther, Mordecai, and the other Jews against their enemies (as always in the LXX, the king is not Ahasuerus, or Xerxes, but Artaxerxes). After a formulaic salutation (E:1; cf. B:1), the king begins an indirect and convoluted self-defense (E:2–14) in an elevated and somewhat bombastic Greek style so reminiscent of chap. B that common authorship is likely. As in B, so here, Artaxerxes modestly stresses his own positive traits. Whereas in the earlier rescript, the emphasis fell on the king's desire to rule fairly and to promote peace and safety (B:2), here it lies on his generosity (E:2–3). This, it turns out, sometimes has the inverse effect of making its beneficiaries so arrogant and resentful that they "scheme against their own benefactors" (v. 3). By taking this position, Artaxerxes makes explicit the burden of the hints in the MT that Haman was insubordinate to his king (see the commentary on 7:8). It is interesting that although chap. A is probably from a different hand, it too makes the same point by associating Haman's rage with Mordecai's foiling of the assassination plot (v. 17). Attributing Haman's disloyalty to his own generosity, Artaxerxes is able not only to distance himself from the genocidal plot but also to continue his posture as the good monarch, committed above all to the well-being of his subjects. Though both the MT and the LXX of Esther leave ample room to doubt the accuracy of the king's self-image, it is nonetheless an image consonant with the tolerant and nonrevolutionary character of the Esther traditions, which see nothing inherently wrong with the phenomenon of Gentile kings ruling Jewish subjects.

But in chap. E Artaxerxes portrays himself as more than just a generous man and good king: He is also shown as a religious person in a way familiar to students of late Second Temple Judaism. He knows, for example, of the "judgment of the God who always sees everything" (v. 4; cf. C:5, 25b) and faults the arrogant who think they can escape it. In fact, rather amazingly, this pagan king even recognizes that "the Jews . . . are governed by very just laws, for they are the children of the Most High, the living God" (E:15–16). In this the author of chap. E follows a long tradition in which foreign dignitaries are made to acknowledge the God of Israel (e.g., Exod. 9:27; 18:10–11; Numbers 22–24; 2 Kings 5:15). In the Second Temple period itself, this tradition became more important, perhaps in compensation for the blows to the Jewish ego wrought by repeated defeat and subjugation to foreign emperors. The portrayal of Artaxerxes in Esther E as one who fears the God of Israel is reminiscent of the portrayal of his predecessor a generation or two earlier, Cyrus, who begins his own pro-Jewish decree by confessing that "the LORD, God of heaven, has given me all the kingdoms of the world and enjoined me to build him a Temple in Jerusalem, which is in Judah" (Ezra 1:2). It is also reminiscent of the emperor Darius's curse at the end of his own rescript confirming Cyrus's: "And may the God who made his name dwell there destroy any king or people who undertakes to alter or to damage that Temple of God which is in Jerusalem" (Ezra 6:12). King Artaxerxes's self-portrayal as sympathetic to the Jews and their God and determined to uproot those who oppose them is consonant with these portraits of earlier Persian emperors in Ezra. It is not so consonant with the portrayal of Ahasuerus in Esther in its MT recension, who seems weak, confused, and quite oblivious to theology altogether, much less to points as particular as the omniscience and judgment of the God of Israel or the special character of his chosen people.

Not surprisingly, chap. E portrays Haman as the diametric opposite of the king, resentful and misanthropic where the latter is generous and benevolent. Moreover, Haman is not even Persian, but Macedonian (v. 10)! The latter designation doubtless reflects the Macedonian king Alexander the Great's defeat of the Persians in 333 B.C.E. and thus serves to make Haman not only an alien, but a secret agent of a nefarious foreign power to boot (v. 14). Just as Artaxerxes's acknowledgment that the Jews "are governed by very just laws" is a repudiation of Haman's charge that "[t]heir laws are different from those of every other people, and they do not keep the king's laws," so is this refashioning of Haman into a seditious alien a repudiation of his characterization of the Jews as "a certain people scattered and unassimilated among all the peoples in all the provinces of Your empire [and] [i]t is not in Your Majesty's interest to leave them alone" (3:8). The villain is once again hoist with his own petard, and the innocent are publicly vindicated.

The orders that Artaxerxes gives in his second rescript include elements that in the MT still lie ahead, suggesting that chap. E may come from a version of Esther somewhat different from that into which it has been spliced. For example, the statement that Haman's household has been impaled with him (v. 18) is at odds with the MT's separation of his impalement from that of his ten sons, with this decree itself falling between the two events (7:10; 9:14). Similarly, Artaxerxes's order to "observe [the 13th of Adar] among your commemorative festivals" (E:22) anticipates Mordecai and Esther's own missives in 9:20–23, 29–32 (the latter designate the 14th and 15th, not the 13th, as the dates of the festival. Perhaps "it" in E:22 means simply "Purim in its appropriate time"). Since the rescript is addressed to the royal governors (v. 1), this command to observe the Jewish festival is strange. It is conceivable that we have here a remnant of the Gentile origin of Purim. More likely, the governors are simply enjoined to respect the observance of the new festival by the Jews, who were mentioned in v. 19.

2. A New Edict Is Issued (continued)
(8:13–14)

8:13 A copy of the writ was to be issued as a decree in every province and publicly displayed to all the peoples, so that the Jews might be ready for that day, to execute vengeance upon their enemies. 14 The couriers rid-

ing swift horses, royal coursers,[a] rushed out posthaste at the king's command, and the decree was issued in the fortified complex of Susa.

a. See the note to 8:10.

This section should be viewed as the continuation of Esther 8:9–12 after the
interruption of chap. E, which, as we saw, sits uneasily in the Masoretic Esther. In other words, 8:9–14 is one unit. The language of v. 13 closely parallels that of 3:14, the only real difference being the emphasis on self-defense in
the case of the Jews ("to execute vengeance upon their enemies"). Hostilities
are initiated by the anti-Semites, not the Jews. Nonetheless, the language here,
which is admittedly ambiguous, may imply, as Paton claims, that the Jews are
now granted "not merely the right of self-defense, but also to do to their enemies as the enemies intend to do to them,"[189] and this is indeed what happens
(9:1–16). As in the case of 3:15, the couriers ride out "posthaste" (8:14),
though here the additional term *mĕbōhālîm* (captured inexactly by the verb
"rushed" in our translation) expresses added urgency. If, with the medieval
Jewish commentator Rashi, we attribute this to the necessity of overtaking the
first set of couriers,[190] it would be better to emend "the third month" in 8:9 to
"the first month," the term that appears in some ancient versions. In that case,
the second set of couriers were dispatched only ten days after the first. All this,
though possible, depends in my judgment upon too particular a motivation for
mĕbōhālîm for the emendation to be necessary.

Despite the great influence of 3:12–15 on 8:9–14, one key element of the
former is unparalleled in the latter: the king and Haman's sitting down to drink
after the genocidal decree went forth and the city of Susa was thrown into pandemonium (3:15). The Jews are wiser than Haman and thus not so confident as
he was. Their feasting will come only when they have attained relief from their
enemies. Whereas his celebration was short-lived, theirs endured and will continue to endure from generation to generation (9:20–23).

3. The Exaltation of Mordecai
and the Happiness of the Jews (8:15–17)

8:15 When Mordecai came out of the king's presence in royal garb of violet and white, wearing an enormous golden crown and a cloak of fine
linen and purple wool, the city of Susa cried out in joy. **16** For the Jews
there were light, joy, happiness, and honor. **17** And in every province and

[189]Paton, 276. Note also Fox, *Character,* 101: " . . . NQM never refers to a simple defense or
rescue, but everywhere designates punitive action and presupposes a prior wrong, that is, some offense to which the avenging party is responding."
[190]Rashi to 8:14.

in every city, wherever the king's command and decree had reached, there were joy and happiness among the Jews, feasting and a holiday, and many among the people of the land identified themselves with the Jews because the fear of the Jews had fallen upon them.

In this passage, we come upon another of the climaxes in the story of the Jews' turning the tables upon their enemies. Verse 15 is the reversal of 4:1, where Mordecai rends his garments and puts on sackcloth and ashes in a public demonstration of his grief about the genocidal order that has just gone forth. Now that the countervailing rescript has been rushed out to the provinces, he goes forth dressed in royal raiment and bearing a gold crown upon his head. Just as Haman's advisers and his wife had predicted, Mordecai's being temporarily clothed in royal garb during the parade in chap. 6 has proven to be an omen (6:11, 13) and, as Paton puts it, "[he] is now privileged to wear continually what before he received for a short time only."[191] His investiture in purple wool is a particularly striking indication of his change in status. When Daniel proves able to decipher the writing on the wall, he, too, is clothed in purple—in order to show that "he shall rule as third [or one of three] in the empire" (Dan. 5:7, 29). Mordecai's new garb similarly shows that he now stands alongside Ahasuerus and Esther in the royal administration. It should also be noticed that the garments and colors mentioned in Esth. 8:15 are reminiscent of the vestments of the priesthood (*kōhănîm*) in the Torah (e.g., Exod. 28:6; cf. 1 Macc. 10:15–20; 59–66). Given the substantial overlap of the royal and the priestly offices in ancient Israel, this is not surprising. But Bardtke is probably right that Mordecai is here viewed as a kind of secular priest celebrated for his service on behalf of his threatened people.[192] The joy with which the city of Susa cries out in Esth. 8:15 is the joy of salvation. It parallels the response of the worshiping community upon learning that their sacrifices have been accepted (cf. Lev. 9:24). The last clause in Esth. 8:15 reverses the last clause of 3:15 ("the city of Susa cried out in joy" versus "the city of Susa was thrown into confusion"). There is no reason to assume, as some commentators have,[193] that only the Jews rejoiced at Mordecai's elevation.

Esther 8:16 is the reversal of 4:3, with the four positive terms of the former ("light, joy, happiness, and honor") contrasting with the four negative terms of the latter ("mourning . . . fasting, weeping, and wailing").[194] It is possible that "light" here refers to feasting (cf. 1 Sam. 14:29) as opposed to the fasting of

[191]Paton, 279.
[192]Bardtke, 374.
[193]E.g., Paton, 280.
[194]Clines, 97.

4:3. It is more certain that the "honor" that the Jews have acquired contrasts with the disgrace that they enacted by putting on sackcloth and ashes in 4:3.[195]

The meaning of the otherwise unattested word *mityahădîm* in 8:17, rendered above as "identified themselves with the Jews," is unclear. It has often been seen to refer to conversion to Judaism, which is a well-attested phenomenon in late Second Temple times. The book of Judith offers support for this interpretation in Achior the Ammonite's conversion to Judaism after Judith's heroism delivers her people from the mortal threat (Judith 14:10). By the time standards for conversion had been worked out in detail (the rabbinic period), the motivation for conversion given here "fear of the Jews"—would be judged invalid, and this is doubtless why the Talmud holds that these would-be converts in Mordecai's day were not accepted by the Jewish authorities.[196] There is no reason, however, that this mysterious verb (the reflexive participle formed from the root of the noun "Jew") need refer to a *religious* change. It may simply indicate that these Gentiles sided with the Jews, fearful of being associated with the anti-Semites, whose star had clearly gone into a fatal eclipse. Perhaps they pretended to be Jewish, just as Esther pretended to be Gentile at first (Esth. 2:10, 20). If so, things have truly come full circle. Whereas the Jews were once threatened and trying to pass as non-Jews, now the Gentiles, feeling endangered by the unexpected consequences of the anti-Semitism in their midst, are passing as Jews, perhaps permanently. The fear that falls upon these Gentiles is yet another instance of the mysterious grace that seems to envelop the Jews throughout this story (see 2:9; 4:14; 5:2; and 6:13).

Clines has constructed an elaborate argument that 8:15–17 once constituted the end of the story of Mordecai and Esther, and chaps. 9–10 have been tacked on.[197] Against this, Fox has argued that even the Alpha Text (AT), which he agrees reflects a pre-Masoretic form of the story, included material about the actual battle (though not about Purim, which seems to have been a later interpolation into the original conclusion of the story).[198] In this connection it should be noted, first, that biblical narratives seldom end at the point of climax but usually wind down, often with more cultic or genealogical material, and second, that any form of Esther that ended without a description of what actually transpired on Adar 13 would be strangely and atypically unsatisfying. As Paton remarks, given two contradictory royal edicts in force, one ordering attacks on the Jews and the other ordering Jewish attacks upon anti-Semites, "[l]ively times are to be anticipated."[199] As we shall see in the next chapter, lively times are indeed to be the order of the day.

[195]*Yosef Leqaḥ* to 8:16.
[196]*b. Yeb.* 24b.
[197]Clines, 26–30.
[198]Fox, *Redaction,* 38–42.
[199]Paton, 282.

IX. The Fateful Three Days

Esther 9:1–32

1. Battle Is Joined—and Renewed (9:1–19)

9:1 In the twelfth month (that is, the month of Adar), on its thirteenth day, when the king's command and decree were to be put into operation, on the day when the enemies of the Jews had expected to overpower them, the reverse occurred: It was the Jews who overpowered their enemies. 2 Throughout all the provinces of King Ahasuerus, the Jews assembled in their cities to lay hands upon those who were seeking to do them harm, and no one could withstand them, for the fear of them had fallen upon all peoples. 3 All the officers of the provinces, the satraps, the governors, and the royal officials gave honor[a] to the Jews because the fear of Mordecai fell upon them. 4 For Mordecai had become a powerful person in the royal palace, and his reputation was spreading through all the provinces, for the man Mordecai was continually growing more powerful.

5 The Jews struck all their enemies with the sword, slaying and annihilating; they did as they pleased with those who hated them. 6 In the fortified compound of Susa, the Jews killed five hundred men and annihilated them. 7 They also slew[b] Parshandatha, Dalphon, Aspatha, 8 Poratha, Adalia, Aridatha, 9 Parmashta, Arisai, Aridai, and Vaizatha 10 —the ten sons of Haman, son of Hammedatha, enemy of the Jews. But they did not lay a hand on the spoil.

11 On that same day the number of those killed in the fortified compound of Susa reached the king. 12 "In the fortified compound of Susa," the king said to Queen Esther, "the Jews have slain and annihilated five hundred men as well as the ten sons of Haman. What must they have done in the rest of the king's provinces! What is your wish? It shall be granted you! What more is your request? It shall be fulfilled!" 13 "If it please Your Majesty," replied Esther, "let it be granted to the Jews in Susa to act again tomorrow according to the decree for today, and let the ten sons of Haman be impaled on the stake." 14 The king ordered that this be done; the decree was issued in Susa; and the ten sons of Haman were impaled.[c] 15 So the Jews in Susa assembled again on the fourteenth of the month of Adar and slew three hundred men in Susa. But they did not lay a hand on the spoil.

16 The rest of the Jews, those in the king's provinces, also assembled and fought for their lives. They obtained relief from their enemies, slaying seventy-five thousand of those who hated them. But they did not lay a hand on the spoil. **17** This was on the thirteenth day of the month of Adar. They rested on the fourteenth and made that into a day of banqueting and merrymaking. **18** But the Jews in Susa assembled on the thirteenth and the fourteenth. They rested on the fifteenth and made that into a day of banqueting and merrymaking. **19** This is why village Jews—those who live in unwalled towns—keep the fourteenth day of the month of Adar in merrymaking and banqueting and as a holiday, sending presents of food to each other.[d]

a. *Mĕnaśśĕ'îm* here may mean "aided," as in Ezra 1:4,[200] but our rendering "gave honor," which is also possible, draws attention to the contrast with 3:1, as explained in the commentary.

b. "They also slew" is transposed from v. 10 for reasons of sense. No emendation is intended.

c. There is much versional support for adding the words "on the stake" (*'al hā'ēṣ*), as in 2:23; 6:4; 7:10; 8:7; 9:13, 25. The sense is not affected.

d. Note that the LXX adds: "but those who dwell in major cities also observe the fifteenth day of Adar as a time of good cheer, sending portions to their neighbors." The contrast of villagers and city people is implicit also in the MT to 9:19, which seems oddly truncated. See the commentary.

Esther 9 can be divided into two broad sections. The first, vv. 1–19, which occupy us here, tells of the final victory of the Jews of the Persian empire over their mortal enemies. The second, vv. 20–32, tells us how these felicitous circumstances gave birth to a continuing and normative Jewish practice, the festival of Purim.

In v. 1, the great theme of reversal, which dominates the entire book, comes at last to explicit statement: "the reverse occurred: It was the Jews who overpowered their enemies." Precisely who these remaining enemies are is unclear, since Haman, who hatched the anti-Semitic plot, has already been dispatched (7:9–10). Too much can be made of this, however, for there have been hints all along of more widespread animosity against the Jews—for example, in Mordecai's instructions that Esther keep her ethnicity secret (2:10, 20), or in the very notion that a royal decree that an entire populace eliminate its Jewish minority could find a receptive ear with the citizenry. The key in v. 1 is not that the Jews acted on their royal authorization "to destroy, slay, and annihilate the armed forces of any people or province that might attack them" (8:11). Here a different verb is used, *šlṭ*, rendered above as "overpower," but with connotations of

[200]See Moore, *Esther*, 86.

rule and authority. The most important aspect of the great battles of Adar 13–14 is thus not the slaughter, by which the Jews turned the tables on the anti-Semites, but rather their assumption of a new status of honor and dominion, symbolized by the accession of one of their own as prime minister in the previous verses (8:15–17). Just as Mordecai and the Jewish community mourned and lamented together at the nadir of their affliction (4:1–3), so they rise to power together in the moment of triumph.

In 9:2, we hear anew the ancient motif of the neighboring nations frightened by the victorious exodus of Israel and cowering at their approach (e.g., Exod. 15:14–16; Josh. 2:8–11; Ps. 105:38). The difference here is that the Gentiles are afraid not of the God of Israel, but of Israel themselves and of their representative, Mordecai (8:17; 9:2, 3). Gerleman is correct to speak of a certain desacralization of holy war in Esther,[201] but this must not be taken to mean that the fear in question was thought to be accounted for by purely naturalistic reasoning. Rather, it is another manifestation of the mysterious charisma that protects the Jews throughout the story. In this instance, the charisma manifests itself, as Clines puts it,[202] in the form of a "numinous dread"—no less numinous for its origin in the desacralization of the triumphal march of the divine warrior in ancient holy war traditions. Clines is also correct to note that the Jews understand Ahasuerus's latest edict as an authorization not only to resist their enemies but to act preemptively against them.[203] He is wrong, however, to interpret 9:2 as saying that the Jews encountered no opposition. Rather, the expression *'îš lō' 'āmad l/bipnê* is better rendered "no one could withstand," as in Josh. 23:9, where it describes the Canaanite kings in the face of the conquest under Joshua. Those kings surely resisted, but to no avail, because of the protective power of YHWH, God of Israel.

One might also note that the diction of 9:2 exhibits points of affinities with that of 2:21 ("to lay hands on those who were seeking to do them harm" [*lišlōaḥ yād bimbaqšê rā'ātām*] and "sought to lay hands on" [*waybaqšû lišlōaḥ yād*]). This suggests another instance of the principle of measure for measure that is so important in our book (see, e.g., the commentary on 7:9–10). Mordecai acts to save the king's life, and then the king acts to save the lives of Mordecai's people. Herein again lies a hint of the seditiousness of anti-Semitism, another ironic twist since Haman's initial accusation against the Jews centered on their alleged disloyalty to the king and his laws (3:8). The same principle can be heard in the verb *mĕnaśśĕ'îm* ("gave honor to") in 9:3. This was the verb that described Ahasuerus's elevation of Haman in 3:1 (*waynaśśĕ'ēhû*). By refusing to recognize that elevation, Mordecai endangered himself and his entire

---

[201]Gerleman, 132.
[202]Clines, 14.
[203]Ibid., 21.

people, but he also ensured his own elevation in place of Haman—and now the elevation of all the Jews as well, at the hands of the very officials formerly charged with their annihilation (3:12–13).

Esther 9:4, which speaks in more summary fashion about Mordecai's ascent, is so close in wording to Exod. 11:3, which tells of Moses' heightened status as the last of the plagues approach, that deliberate patterning can be reasonably suspected. The verse in Esther consists of three brief clauses (four words in the first and last, three in the intermediate clause, counting joined words as one in all cases). It begins and ends with the same word (*gādôl,* "powerful"), which thus further links the first and third clauses.[204] This word again connects Mordecai's magnification with that of Haman, whom Ahasuerus "promoted" (*giddal*) in 3:1. The word *hôlēk* ("spreading," "growing") is common to the second clause and the third.[205] These two significant terms draw together the three clauses in this artfully constructed little verse by standing next to each other at its finale: the Jew "was continually growing more powerful" (*hôlēk wĕgādôl*). Note, finally, that the term "man," applied to Mordecai here, recalls his introduction in 2:5, where he was described as *'îš yĕhûdî* (literally, "a Jewish man"), thus drawing attention to the contrast between his status as a mere exile there and his elevation to great power here.[206]

Whereas Esth. 9:1–4 offers a general summary, vv. 5–19 provide the gory details. When one reads the account of the bloodshed, it is important not to lose sight of the murderousness of the victims. These are not ordinary townsmen, but enemies of the Jews who had fully expected, as 9:1 points out, to overpower the Jews on the day selected for the genocide. As André LaCocque astutely puts it, "[t]he Jewish victory in Susa is equivalent to a successful insurrection in the World War II-era Warsaw ghetto with the result of 75,000 S.S. troops being slaughtered."[207] In this connection, the special attention given Haman's ten sons in vv. 7–10 is doubly fitting: first, because of Haman's boast to his wife and advisers about the great number of his sons (5:11), and second, because of his Amalekite extraction and the concomitant obligation on the Jews to eliminate altogether this tribe of brutal and implacable enemies (Exod. 17:8–16; Deut. 25:17–19; cf. the commentary on 2:5 and 3:1). The long list of the names of the sons (9:7–9) recalls the list of the names of the king's advisers and of his attending eunuchs (1:10, 14) and, like those lists, provides a sense of historical accuracy (whether valid or not) and perhaps of comedy as well. Note that 9:7, 8, and 9 all begin with a name that starts with *p,* is accented on

---

[204]Hakham, 56. Note also that the first and last clauses both begin with *kî* ("for").

[205]Bardtke, 382.

[206]Ehrlich (*Randglossen,* 1:301) makes the point that the word *'îš* with a proper name implies importance, as in Num. 12:3; Judg. 17:5; and Dan. 9:21.

[207]André LaCocque, *The Feminine Unconventional,* OBT, Minneapolis, 1990, 80 n. 64.

the penultimate syllable (which always has an *a* vowel), and ends with *t(h)a*. The first two verses give three names and the last gives four, for a further climactic effect.[208] In the public cantillation of Esther in the synagogue on the night and morning of Purim, these ten sons are given especially short shrift: The reader must recite all ten names in one breath![209] That the Jews "did not lay a hand on the spoil" (v. 10) stands in conspicuous contrast with Saul's conduct in war against the Amalekite king Agag in 1 Samuel 15. Mordecai rises on the very point on which Saul fell.

Ahasuerus's response to the massacre inside the fortified compound (Esth. 9:12) reveals yet again his insensitivity and obtuseness. As Fox puts it, "[h]e seems impressed, perhaps bemused, by the death toll more than by the Jews' deliverance."[210] This befits, one might add, both his concentration on the physical and his grandiosity. His question to Esther repeats the gist of 5:3, 6; 7:2, although in a mode more of comedy than of high drama, since, as he acknowledges, the outcome is not exactly in doubt. The second part of her answer, a request that the ten sons of Haman be impaled (9:13), may seem out of place since v. 10 has already reported their deaths. It is possible that the exchange in vv. 12–13 derives, in whole or in part, from a different source, which does not know the previous report of the slaughter of Haman's sons. But, as the contrast of v. 10 with v. 6 suggests, unlike the other enemies in the fortified compound, Haman's sons had been only killed, not "annihilated." Esther's request is not for their execution but for their public disgrace through the exposure of their corpses, a well-attested practice in antiquity, especially when the victims have been charged with insurrection (cf. Josh. 8:29; 10:26; 1 Sam. 31:10; Herodotus 3:125; 6:30).[211] By seeking a renewal of the king's authorization of war for another day as well as permission to display the corpses of the chief anti-Semite's heirs, Esther is demonstrating that the Jews' actions are strictly in accordance with state policy. As Craig notes, "[a]n ironic point reinforces the change of affairs: in the course of the vignette [of Esth. 9:11–15] we learn that, despite Haman's objections, these people *do* keep and abide by the king's laws (cf. 3:8)."[212]

Esther 9:15, in which the Susan Jews act upon the king's renewed authorization, provides the basis for an etiology of Shushan Purim, the celebration of the festival of Purim a day later (i.e., on the fifteenth of Adar) in Susa (see 9:18) and, according to the later rabbinic legislation, in any city that was walled in the time of Joshua as well.[213] The difference in practice between the Jews of the capital and those everywhere else in the empire is the principal theme of

---

[208]Hakham, 58.
[209]See *b. Meg.* 16b.
[210]Fox, *Character,* 112.
[211]Paton, 287.
[212]Craig, *Reading Esther,* 130.
[213]*b. Meg.* 2a–3b.

vv. 16–19. One can suspect that Paton is right that "[h]istory here arises from custom, not custom from history"[214] and that the difference in date actually has some other origin. In this connection, note that 9:20–22 can (but does not have to) be understood as requiring *all* the Jews to observe *both* days. Finally, it should not be missed that whereas the book of Esther presents Adar 13 as the day of the great battle against the anti-Semites, other Jewish literature reports that this was the day on which Judah Maccabee's forces slew the Seleucid general Nicanor, seizing spoil and cutting off his head and right hand for public display in Jerusalem (1 Macc. 7:43–49; 2 Macc. 15:28–37). A rabbinic source continues to consider this a feast day, the "Day of Nicanor,"[215] though post-Talmudic Jewish tradition makes it into the opposite, the "Fast of Esther," which is still observed today. 2 Maccabees 15:36 reports that Adar 13 is "the day before Mordecai's Day," though it must remain unclear what exactly the author thinks happened on the latter and what, if anything, is the connection of the Day of Nicanor to the events in the book of Esther.[216]

Esther 9:16–17 does not follow v. 15 chronologically, but instead supplements the summary given in vv. 1–4 (and perhaps v. 5). The shift in focus is somewhat confusing and may be owing to less than ideal redaction. The overall effect, however, is to convey a vivid sense of Jewish solidarity despite differences in time and place. The form of the verbs in v. 16b (the infinitive absolute) argues that this sentence belongs with the following verse rather than with v. 16a,[217] as the text transitions nicely into the subject of Purim, which will occupy the rest of the chapter. The etiological note that is v. 19 may be a late expansion of the etiology of the differences in the dates of Purim provided in vv. 11–15, since now the contrast is no longer limited to that between Susa and everywhere else but has been changed into a contrast between Jews in villages and, presumably, those in large cities. This is explicit in the LXX, which adds a clause noting that the latter Jews observe the *fifteenth* of Adar. In the MT to v. 19, and even more so in the LXX version of it, we may be seeing the scripturalization of an evolution in practice toward what was eventually to become the rabbinic institution of Shushan Purim, the celebration of Purim on Adar 15 in *all* cities walled from the time of Joshua, not just Susa itself.

Esther 9:19 details two of the practices that rabbinic tradition would interpret as mandatory for the observance of Purim, a festive banquet and the exchange of gifts. The rabbis see those gifts (*mānôt*) as food, an interpretation for which there is indeed biblical warrant (1 Sam. 1:5; 9:23). The closest analogy

---

[214]Paton, 288.

[215]See *b. Ta'an* 18b.

[216]The idea that the story of Nicanor lies behind the events of the book of Esther is intriguing but too speculative to accept. See Roger Herst, "The Purim Connection," *USQR* 28 (1973): 139–45; rpt. in Moore, *Studies,* 220–26.

[217]Paton, 289–90.

to the practice in Esth. 9:19 is found in Neh. 8:10–12, in which Ezra and Ne-hemiah urge the Jews of Jerusalem to eat rich foods and drink sweet beverages, to be in good spirits, and to send presents (*mānôt*) to those who have nothing prepared on the first of the seventh month (known in later rabbinic tradition as Rosh Hashanah, the fall New Year's festival). This could suggest that the send-ing of gifts in Esth. 9:19 is for the benefit of the needy, but v. 22 distinguishes between these "presents of food to each other and gifts to the poor" and man-dates both practices. They have remained essential features of Purim ever since.

Note that the first mention of the bestowing of presents in Esther occurs in 2:9, when Hegai the harem-keeper provides Esther, who has caught his fancy, with "delicacies" (*mānôt*). Since this term can also have the connotation of "al-lotted portion" (e.g., Ps. 16:5), its use in connection with Purim, the Festival of Lots, is deeply appropriate. The Jews are to continue extending to each other the generous lot that Esther received at the hands of Hegai and then shared with her kinsmen through her own intervention with Ahasuerus. It is unlikely, how-ever, that the term *mānôt* somehow reflects the actual etymology of Purim as the Festival of Lots (see commentary on 9:24–26a).[218]

2. Purim Instituted, Confirmed, and Reconfirmed (9:20–32)

9:20 Mordecai recorded these things and sent letters to all the Jews, near and far, throughout all the provinces of King Ahasuerus, **21** enjoining them to keep the fourteenth day of the month of Adar and the fifteenth, every year, **22** as the days on which the Jews obtained relief from their enemies and the month that had been transformed for them from a time of grief to one of joy, and from an occasion of mourning to a holiday. They were to keep them as days of banqueting and joy, sending presents of food to each other and gifts to the poor. **23** Thus the Jews undertook[a] to continue the customs that they had begun to keep and about which Mordecai had written to them. **24** For Haman, son of Hammedatha, the enemy of all the Jews, had plotted to annihilate the Jews and had cast *pur* (which means "the lot") with the intention of discomfiting and annihi-lating them. **25** But when the matter[b] came to the king's attention, he is-sued a written edict that the evil plot that he had devised against the Jews recoil on his own head and that he and his sons be impaled upon a stake. **26** Therefore, these days were named "Purim," after the word *pur*.

Accordingly, because of all the instructions in the aforesaid letter, and because of all that they had experienced in that affair and how it turned

[218]Contra Gerleman, 26–27.

out for them, 27 the Jews resolved and irrevocably undertook, on behalf of themselves, their descendants, and all who might join them, that they would keep these two days in the prescribed manner and at their appointed time every year; 28 that these days would be remembered and kept in every generation and by every family in every province and every city and that these days of Purim would never leave the midst of the Jews nor the memory of them cease among their descendants.

29 Then Queen Esther, daughter of Abihail, and Mordecai the Jew, wrote with full authority[c] to confirm this second[d] letter about Purim. 30 Letters conveying wishes of peace and faithfulness were sent to all the Jews in the one hundred twenty-seven provinces of Ahasuerus's empire 31 in order to make these days of Purim obligatory in their appointed times, just as Mordecai the Jew and Queen Esther had prescribed and just as they had accepted for themselves and their descendants the obligations of fasts and lamentation. 32 Esther's command confirmed these rules for Purim, and it is preserved in writing.

a. Reading the plural *wĕqibbĕlû,* with several Masoretic manuscripts, the LXX, and by analogy to the *qĕrê* of 9:27.

b. The subject of the infinitive (*bō'āh*), indicated by its feminine possessive suffix, is unclear. See the commentary. As rendered here, the antecedent is *maḥăšebet,* "plot."

c. *'Et-kol-tōqep,* here translated "with full authority," is awkward and obscure. One would have expected to see *b* instead of *'ēt* as the preposition if this is the correct sense. The emendations that have been proposed for this verse are legion. The least radical suggestion is Fox's that *tōqep* ("authority") be taken as "a trope for *words* of authority" so that "Esther (or she and Mordecai) put into writing the authority necessary to validate the observance."[219] On the problem of the verse in general, see our commentary.

d. *Haššēnît* is missing in the Greek, but it is not necessary to delete it to make sense of the verse. See the commentary.

Esther 9:20–32 provides a set of etiologies of Purim in the narrower sense of the legal mechanisms by which the Jews became obligated in perpetuity to observe this new, post-Pentateuchal holiday. The text exhibits enough inconcinnities, redundancies, and obscurities as to provide additional evidence for its secondary character and for a complicated redactional history behind the association of Purim with the tale of Esther and Mordecai (see the commentary on 8:15–17, end).

Though Jewish tradition has often seen a reference to the book of Esther itself in the statement that "Mordecai recorded these things" (9:20),[220] the more

---

[219]Fox, *Character,* 286.
[220]E.g., Rashi to 9:20.

likely interpretation is that Mordecai included a summary of the key events in the letters he sent to the Jews to enjoin them to observe the fourteenth and the fifteenth of Adar as days of festival. "Near and far" may be derived from Isa. 57:19, in which YHWH announces "well-being, well-being upon the far and the near" and promises to heal them.[221] If so, then the implication is that in the events that have led to the institution of Purim, the Jews are to see the fulfillment of an ancient prophecy of deliverance. The verb *qiyyēm,* rendered as "enjoining" in Esth. 9:21, appears late in the history of biblical Hebrew and is cognate with Aramaic *qĕyāmā',* which translates the biblical words for "covenant" and "oath." The parallel with the Pentateuchal story is striking: dramatic events of deliverance (the exodus and the events of Adar 13) culminate in a solemn affirmation by the redeemed to accept new obligations upon themselves (the commandments of Sinai, the annual observance of Purim). Esther 9:21 can be understood to imply a two-day festival, in contradiction to the distinction made in 9:19, which would in that case be most likely a later interpolation. But v. 21 can also be understood to mean that in the aggregate the Jews observe both days, with villagers observing the fourteenth and Susans the fifteenth.

The mention of "days" and "month" in v. 22 reflects Haman's original casting of lots "concerning each day and each month" (3:7). The conversion of grief into joy, and of mourning into a holiday is another echo of prophetic predictions of salvation (e.g., Isa. 61:3; Jer. 31:13).[222] What the Jews are to celebrate is not the victory itself; were this the case, Purim would fall on the thirteenth and fourteenth. Rather, they are to celebrate the "relief [they obtained] from their enemies" (Esth. 9:22). The verb that designates this "relief" (*nāḥû*) recalls Haman's words to Ahasuerus in the verse that follows his casting of lots to determine the date of the annihilation of the Jews: "It is not in Your Majesty's interest to leave them alone (*lĕhannîḥām*)" (3:8). Now the Jews are at long last able to be left alone, having survived Haman's nefarious plot and eliminated him and his sympathizers. The mention of "gifts to the poor" in 9:22 is not found in the parallel account of observances given in vv. 17–19, but it does conform to a long-standing Jewish tradition of including the less fortunate and the vulnerable in celebrations (e.g., Deut. 16:11; Tobit 2:1–2). Esther 9:23 indicates an acceptance on the part of the Jews of the obligation to continue to observe Purim, which began with their own spontaneous celebrations but became official with Mordecai's encyclicals (v. 20). This note of popular ratification of an official proclamation stands in marked contrast with the imperiousness to which the Persian regime issues *its* edicts and suggests that the solidarity of the Jews with Mordecai surpasses that of the rest of the Persians with Ahasuerus.

[221]*Yosef Leqaḥ* to 9:20.
[222]Gerleman, 138.

Esther 9:24–26a, a summary of the essential point of the whole story of the book, is so highly compressed that it seems cryptic. In its present location this passage functions as the content of "these things" that Mordecai recorded in the letters he sent to all the Jews (v. 20). Yet doubts have been expressed, most eloquently by Clines, about the conformity of this ostensible summary to the story in the form we now have it.[223] It has also been noted that "discomfiting" in v. 24 seems odd; we expect to see the familiar phrase "to destroy, slay, and annihilate" (e.g., as in 3:13).[224] This difference is most likely owing to a pun on "discomfiting them" (*lĕhummām*) and "Haman" (*hāmān*),[225] and no source distinction need be inferred from it. Clines is correct that the casting of the *pûr* "plays such a minor role in ch. 3 that, from the perspective of that chapter, it probably deserves no place at all in any two-sentence summary of the whole narrative."[226] If, on the other hand, the context is Mordecai's encyclical enjoining the observance of Purim, this minor detail becomes essential, as it is here. Verse 25 displays an awkwardness of phrasing and an obscurity that are uncharacteristic of the book of Esther. The subject of "came" being feminine, one thinks first of Queen Esther's perilous approach to the king in chap. 5. But Esther's name, oddly enough, never appears in 9:24–26a, and without supplying it *ad sensum*, one would best read "plot" (a feminine noun) as the antecedent of the feminine subject here—though even this is syntactically less than satisfying. In addition, v. 25 concentrates only on the figure of Haman and presents the danger as obviated when the king "issued a written edict" (*'āmar 'im hassēper*, another awkward expression) that Haman and his sons be impaled. But the rest of Esther mentions no such written edict; instead, it concentrates on two entirely different documents, the one that ordered the Jews' destruction (3:12–15) and the one that authorized Jewish counteraction against their enemies (8:9–14). Neither of these is mentioned explicitly in 9:24–26a. If we understand the first of these to be implicit in the allusion to Haman's plot in v. 24, then we should probably read v. 25 as implying that the king rescinded the first decree—in blatant contradiction to 8:8. Finally, it should be noted that, as Clines again puts it, "the summary gives the impression that Haman and his sons were impaled at the same time, whereas in the narrative some months have intervened between the two events" (7:9–10; 9:7–9, 13–14)—though, as he concedes, "[t]he compression of the two events is understandable in a summary."[227]

On balance, Clines has made a strong case for the secondary character of 9:24–26a and its derivation from a significant variant of the story that is now

---

[223]Clines, 51–52.
[224]Bardtke, 394.
[225]Hakham, 61.
[226]Clines, 53.
[227]Ibid.

known from chaps. 1–8. Nonetheless, the presence of this summary in Mordecai's official letter makes sense of the differences in ways that we miss if we
ignore this context (which may not have been the original context of the verse).
In particular, by omitting all mention of the king's own involvement in the plot,
the summary demonstrates anew Mordecai's diplomatic skill.[228] To have mentioned this would have been to risk alienating Mordecai's new patron and
incriminating large segments of the Persian population in the anti-Semitic
program. Instead, Mordecai concentrates on one man, Haman, and his sons,
and presents the king as counteracting him definitively and immediately. Note
that this interpretation of the events moves in the direction that eventuates in
chap. E, in which, as we have seen, the king presents himself as altogether on
the side of the good, and Haman as a seditious foreigner attempting to undermine Persia to the benefit of Macedonia.

The naming of the holiday "Purim," though explained in 9:26a, remains
opaque nonetheless. If this is a plural of the word *pûr,* we are left wondering
why, since only one lot was cast. It also remains odd that the lot-casting, which
is mentioned in exactly one verse (3:7), should have become the name of the
festival that commemorates the entire episode. The likelihood is that the word
pûrîm and the festival itself have another origin, one independent of the book
of Esther. Like so many other institutions, these also have been reinterpreted,
reshaped, and revalorized as they have come into Judaism. It is curious that the
earliest reference to Adar 14 outside Esther calls it not "Purim," but the "Day
of Mordecai" (2 Macc. 15:36). One might perhaps speculate that the latter was
the original name of the holiday and that it survived in popular speech even after the effort to identify the day with the originally independent feast of Purim.

The repetition of *'al-kēn* ("therefore, accordingly") in Esth. 9:26 seems
awkward and has often aroused a suspicion of dittography. Rather than in-
dulging in conjectural emendation, however, we can see in the second *'al-kēn*
the beginning of another paragraph, vv. 26b–28. Whereas vv. 24–26a constitute a paraphrase of Mordecai's account of the events, the new paragraph re-
verts to the perspective of the narrator, who as one would expect puts the matter into a more encompassing historical framework. Thus this second summary
stresses not only the Jews' acceptance of the holiday, which v. 23 had already
reported, but also that their action rendered its observance obligatory upon
"their descendants, and all who might join them" (v. 27). The latter group is
designated by a different term from the one that appeared in 8:17 (*nilwîm* as
opposed to *mityahădîm*). Whereas *mityahădîm* is unparalleled in Hebrew (see
the commentary on 8:17), *nilwîm* is a form of a word that appears in late biblical Hebrew as a designation of a convert or something close to it (cf. Isa. 14:1;
56:3, 6). Since Esth. 9:27 looks forward rather than backward, it is unlikely that

[228]Fox, *Character,* 120.

nilwîm here can provide additional backing for the interpretation of *mityahădîm* as being converts in 8:17 (where we have translated it "identified themselves with the Jews").[229] The point is that converts to Judaism through-out the ages are to be obligated to observe Purim, even though they had no Jew-ish biological ancestors at the time of the events that the holiday commemo-rates. This emphasis on futurity and irreversibility is nicely conveyed by the term *wĕlō' ya'ăbôr*, rendered above as "irrevocably" (9:27). These words found toward the end of the book of Esther also appeared toward its beginning, in connection with the promulgation of Ahasuerus's first decree, banishing Vashti (1:19, where they were translated "so that it will not be revoked"; cf. 8:8). The irrevocability of the laws of the Persians and the Medes, which had always seemed so arbitrary and had so endangered Jewish survival, is now invoked for the opposite purpose: to ensure the survival of Purim and the perpetual memory of the dangers that the Jews of Mordecai and Esther's day overcame. Now it is "these days of Purim [that will] never leave (*lō' ya'abrû*) the midst of the Jews" (9:28), even when the grandeur and the buffoonery of the Persian court have long vanished.

Esther 9:28 is noteworthy not only for its legal, formulaic style, but also for its twofold invocation of memory, once at the beginning of the verse and once at the end. It should not be overlooked that the Hebrew root *zkr*, from which the words "remembered" and "memory" here are derived, can have a conno-tation of ritual observance (e.g., Exod. 13:3; 20:8; cf. Deut. 5:12).[230]

It is difficult to quarrel with Clines's judgment that "[v]erses 27–28 have evidently brought the book to a solemn and rhetorically satisfying conclusion; v. 29 is an unexpected resumption of the narrative."[231] It is, in addition, a most confusing verse and one that introduces a passage that is so convoluted and contradictory that conjectural emendations of the text have become legion.[232] That Queen Esther would write a second letter about Purim to confirm the first, which is Mordecai's (vv. 20–22), would make much sense. This would bring the "full authority" of her royal office behind the novel holiday that her cousin had enjoined upon the Jewish community, and it would help restore the bal-ance between Esther and Mordecai that has been characteristic of the narrative from the time the two heroes were introduced in chap. 2 (note that the queen has not been mentioned since 8:7). The first problem is that as v. 29 stands, however, Mordecai coauthors the letter, thus confirming his own previous mis-sive. The second problem is that the wording of the verse tells us that what Esther and Mordecai confirmed is "this second letter about Purim," as if their letter confirmed itself. As Fox observes, "[g]iven the great emphasis the chapter

[229]Contra Fox, *Character*, 121–22.
[230]Ehrlich, 124.
[231]Clines, 55.
[232]See the helpful discussion and charts in Fox, *Character*, 123–28.

places on confirmation and reconfirmation, it is not impossible that this additional validation—a complex self-confirmation—was indeed the author's intention" (though as he acknowledges, difficulties remain nonetheless).[233] It is
also conceivable that "this second letter about Purim" refers to Mordecai's
epistle (vv. 20–22), the first one having been Ahasuerus's edict authorizing
Jewish hostilities against their enemies on Adar 13 (8:9–13). The difficulty
here is that the king's edict nowhere mentions the word "Purim" or even the
concept of a holiday. Or could it be that the author of 9:29 knew the royal edict
in a form that did mention the holiday, as is indeed the case in the version that
is chap. E (vv. 21–23)?

The cleanest solution to the conundrum of 9:29 is to assume that the word
order has gotten a bit jumbled and that the verse means to say this: Queen Esther and Mordecai the Jew, invoking the full authority of their respective offices, wrote a second letter to confirm the observance of Purim.

If the letters described in vv. 30–31 are copies of the one mentioned in v.
29, we have another example of what Fox calls "a complex self-confirmation,"
since the missives are again confirming themselves. The problem can be
avoided with the assumption that these letters are not those of Mordecai and
Esther referred to in v. 31, but rather royal rescripts validating the letters that
these two Jews had already sent. The explicit mention of "the one hundred
twenty-seven provinces of Ahasuerus's empire" in v. 30 may add some slight
support to this interpretation (cf. 8:9; E:21–23). Note, in addition, that whereas
Mordecai and Esther drew up the authorization of Jewish military action in the
king's name (8:8), the authorization of Purim itself has so far come only in their
own names and may therefore have seemed to lack the authority requisite to
establish the new holiday as an irrevocable institution. The notion that the Persian emperor would authorize rules internal to the Jewish community finds a
good parallel in Artaxerxes's commissioning of Ezra to order the affairs of Judah and Jerusalem according to the law of Ezra's God (Ezra 7:14, 25–26).

The mention of "wishes of peace and faithfulness" (*dibrê šālôm we'ĕmet*)
in Esth. 9:30 has been shown to be an echo of the clause, "love faithfulness and
peace" (*wĕhā'ĕmet wĕhaššālôm 'ĕhābû*) in Zech. 8:19, with the inversion of
terms characteristic of intrabiblical citations.[234] The context in Zechariah is the
transformation of days of fasting and mourning into joyful holidays. This is, of
course, very much the point of Purim, and apart from the specific association
of Esth. 9:30 with Zech. 8:19, the language of other verses in Esther (e.g., 8:16)
bears striking similarity to the prophecy of redemption in Zech. 8:19. This argues that the author of Esth. 9:29–32 may have seen a fulfillment of ancient
prophecy in the events narrated in the book to which he appended this passage.

---

[233]Fox, *Character,* 124.
[234]Michael Fishbane, *Biblical Interpretation in Ancient Israel,* Oxford, 1985, 503–5.

The reference to "the obligations of fasts and lamentation" at the end of v. 31 may in fact refer to the four fast days associated with the destruction of Jerusalem mentioned in Zech. 8:19. Just as the Jews had accepted these days upon themselves without a scriptural basis, so would they accept Purim on the authority of Mordecai, Esther, and perhaps an independent royal rescript as well, if that is what 9:30–31 reports.[235] But even if Esth. 9:31 does not continue the allusion to Zech. 8:19, it may still make an analogy between the origin of public fasts and that of Purim. It could be that the public fast in question is actually that of the Susan Jews on behalf of Esther, which they presumably accepted at Esther and Mordecai's behest (Esth. 4:16–17), just as they are now asked to accept Purim. There is no reason, however, to believe that the reference is to the Fast of Esther (*Ta'anit Esther*), a Jewish observance of post-Talmudic origin.

"Esther's command" confirming the rules of Purim (9:32) is also puzzling, since she has nowhere issued a missive in her own name alone. Perhaps we are to see in this a reference to yet another set of letters. Alternately, one can take v. 32 as additional evidence for the secondary insertion of the words "and Mordecai the Jew" in v. 29, so that Esther did indeed issue a Purim letter solely on her own authority—the letter reported in v. 29. If one does keep the name of Mordecai in v. 29, there is a nice balance and symmetry in 9:20–32: Mordecai alone (vv. 20, 23)—Esther and Mordecai (v. 29)—Mordecai and Esther (v. 31)—Esther alone (v. 32). There is another nice touch to the expression Esther's "command" (*ma'ămar*), a term that we have now seen for the third time. The first was in the context of Vashti's refusal to execute "the command (*ma'ămar*) of King Ahasuerus" (1:15). The second time was the notice that "Esther continued to do what Mordecai told her (*ma'ămar*)" (2:20). We have gone from a disobedient queen who is on the receiving end of a command that is not observed, to an obedient queen who is able to issue a command that is observed. The paradox is this: Vashti's insubordination renders her powerless; Esther's subordination renders her powerful.

The pattern of "confirmation and reconfirmation" of Purim in 9:20–32 bespeaks the difficulty of establishing a new holiday, one that lacks authorization in the Torah of Moses or in the mouth of any prophet. The parallel that comes to mind first is the variety of attempts to establish Chanukkah as an annual festival celebrating the Maccabean rededication of the altar in the Temple in Jerusalem (1 Macc. 4:56–59; 2 Macc. 10:1–8). Note that like Purim, Chanukkah was endorsed in letters issued by Jewish authorities to their kinsmen (2 Macc. 1:1–10a; 1:10b–2:18). Still it should not be overlooked that other festivals, celebrating other dramatic redemptive events, failed to be established, or once established failed to survive (e.g., 1 Macc. 7:49; 13:49–52;

---

[235]See Ibn Ezra to 9:30.

3 Macc. 6:30–36). The redundant and convoluted character of Esth. 9:20–32 may reflect a series of difficulties that the advocates of the new holiday—or the new revalorization of an older, popular holiday—faced over a period of years.

X. The Greatness of Ahasuerus and Mordecai

Esther 10:1–3

10:1 King Ahasuerus imposed tribute on the mainland and on the islands. 2 All that he did with authority and might and the story of the high position to which the king promoted Mordecai are inscribed in the Annals of the Kings of Media and Persia. 3 For Mordecai the Jew ranked second to King Ahasuerus. He was the most powerful of the Jews and highly regarded by the multitude of his kinsmen. He continually sought the good of his people and spoke in behalf of the welfare of his kindred.

Esther 10:1 seems out of place. As Clines observes, it "has the air of an introduction to a narrative that is summarily truncated,"[236] and the possibility exists that a sentence dealing with Ahasuerus in some other document has made its way into Esther. The absence of the verse, and of all of chap. 10, in the Alpha Text may speak to the same point. Even so, however, the report of Ahasuerus's tribute makes some sense within the story into which it has been spliced. The act here reported is the reverse of the remission of taxes that the king proclaimed when he selected Esther as his new queen (2:18).[237] Things have now regained equilibrium, and whatever sacrifice the crown made because of Esther has now been recouped in grand style. In addition, there may be a connection with Haman's offer to bribe the king to authorize his program of genocide (3:9). As Moore puts it, "[a]lthough the crown presumably had not gained the ten thousand talents promised by Haman in return for the pogrom, Mordecai convinced the king that peaceful taxation rather than plundering was the best way to fill the royal coffers."[238] In any event, the report of Ahasuerus's augmented revenue after his promotion of Mordecai is a further indication of the wisdom of the deed, and it redounds to the credit of both men. (Note the parallel report of the benefit to Pharaoh of Joseph's administration as prime minister of Egypt in Gen. 47:13–26.)[239]

---

[236]Clines, 57.

[237]Ehrlich, 125.

[238]Moore, *Esther,* 98–99. See David Daube, "The Last Chapter of Esther," *JQR* 37 (1946–47): 139–47.

[239]Fox, *Character,* 129.

Esther 10:2–3 elaborates on the theme of the greatness of Mordecai that dominates 9:1–4; it could conceivably derive from a story of Mordecai independent of the tale of Esther, who is conspicuous for her absence in chap. 10. The reference to the king's promotion of the Jew (*giddĕlô*) again recalls the use of the same term in connection with Haman (10:2; 3:1; 5:11). The only other appearance of the word *pārāšâ* ("story") in Esther—or in the whole Hebrew Bible—is in 4:7, where Mordecai indirectly tells Esther "the story of the money that Haman had offered to deposit in the royal treasury in exchange for the destruction of the Jews." Now things have altogether reversed themselves, and the story of the money that was paid to destroy the Jews for Mordecai's refusal to bow has become the story of the king's successful imposition of taxes and of Mordecai's power and grandeur. The inscription of this new situation in the royal annals of Media and Persia accomplishes two things. First, by referring the reader to the official annals of the empire, 10:2 vouches for the authenticity of the whole preceding narrative and further guarantees the normativity of the new holiday, Purim. Second, the same act of writing endows the new situation with a measure of permanence parallel to the permanence of Purim that comes from Mordecai and Esther's own setting of the events and the new norms into writing (9:20–22, 29). As L. Hindy Najman puts it:

> If, as in the Joseph story, a new king should arise who is unfamiliar with the history of Jewish service to the throne (Exodus 1:8), that king will be reminded, as was Achashverosh [i.e., Ahasuerus] (6:2), by the permanent written record of the written chronicles. Thus, the *Esther* narrative is established as a precedent and the power of writing will continue to protect the Jews against future enemies.[240]

The Masoretic Esther closes where it opened, with a report of the authority and might of King Ahasuerus (1:1–9; 10:1–2)—except that the conclusion includes a new element, the greatness of Mordecai the Jew. As "the most powerful of the Jews" (*gādôl layyĕhûdîm*), he is the diametric opposite of the man he replaced, Haman, "the enemy of the Jews" (*ṣōrēr hayyĕhûdîm*, 3:10; 8:1; 9:10, 24). His popularity among "the multitude of his kinsmen" (*rōb 'eḥāyw*, 10:3) contrasts with Haman's boast about "his many sons" (*rōb bānāyw*, 5:11): The sons all perished in the Jewish counterstrike against the anti-Semitic conspiracy of their father, whereas the Jews continue to live and to thrive under the effective guidance of their leader, Mordecai. The scene with which the Masoretic Esther closes is one for which Jewish communities in the Diaspora have always longed: Jews

---

[240]L. Hindy Najman, "The Representation of Writing in *Esther*," paper for Prof. Peter B. Machinist's class in "History and Historiography in the Ancient Near East," Harvard University, January, 1992, 10.

living in harmony and mutual goodwill with the Gentile majority, under Jewish leaders who are respected and admired by the rulers, yet who are openly identified with the Jewish community and unashamed to advance its interests and to speak out in its defense.

Matters Concluded

Chapter F:1–11 (= Esther 10:4–11:1 in the Vulgate)

1. Mordecai's Premonition Decoded (F:1–10)

F:1 *Mordecai said, "These things are God's doing, 2 for I remember the dream in which I saw these things, and not one of the visions has been left unfulfilled— 3 the small spring that became a river, the light, the sun, the many waters. The river is Esther, whom the king married and made queen. 4 The two dragons are myself and Haman. 5 The nations are those who assembled to annihilate the name of the Jews. 6 As for my nation, it is Israel, who cried out to God and were delivered.*

For the Lord *has delivered his people and rescued us from all those evils. God has worked great signs and wonders such as have never occurred among the nations. 7 For this purpose he made two lots, one for the people of God and one for all the nations. 8 These two lots came to be fulfilled in the hour, the time, and the day of judgment before God and among all the nations. 9 For God remembered his people and rendered justice for his inheritance.*

10 Therefore, they shall celebrate these days on the fourteenth and fifteenth of the month of Adar by gathering together in joy and gladness before God throughout all generations of his people Israel, forever.

Like its Masoretic forebear, the Septuagint Esther ends on a note that recalls its beginning. Esther F:1–10, the bulk of the last of the six "Apocryphal additions to Esther," is a decoding of chap. A, Mordecai's apocalyptic dream. The "great river" of A:9 is Esther (F:3); the two dragons "readied for combat" in A:5 are Mordecai himself and Haman (F:4), and the "race of the just" terrified by the preparations for war of "every people" (A:6, 8) are the Jews beset by "[t]he nations" (F:5).

Despite Mordecai's claim that "not one of the visions has been left unfulfilled" (F:2), the decoding is fragmentary and forced in places. For example, the "small spring," the "light," and the "sun" of A:9–10 are never explained but, apparently, all assimilated to the "great river" that is Esther. One could imagine a fuller interpretation: The small spring is Esther in her first appearance, as a vulnerable beauty queen, before her transformation into a great river (that is, a regal figure skilled in rhetoric and diplomacy, who successfully defeats the enemy of her people and takes possession of his estate to boot). As for the "light," note that even in the MT this is the possession of the Jews after the king's second edict has been promulgated (8:16). The sunlight breaking through represents the deliverance of the Jews and could conceivably be interpreted to refer more specifically to the "enormous golden crown" that Mordecai wore when he left the critical meeting with the king (8:15). These possibilities for a fuller and more satisfactory decoding are not taken. On the other hand, the interpretation of Mordecai himself as a dragon (F:4) is awkward, for dragons tend to represent the primordial and eschatological enemies of God,[241] and not heroes. In this connection, note that in A:5–6, it is a cry from *both* dragons that brings about the afflictions of the righteous. One could argue that this symbolizes Mordecai's provocation of the whole crisis by refusing to bow to Haman (3:1–6), and perhaps this is what the decoding in chap. F and the prefixing of chap. A to an older form of the book of Esther had in mind. But, even so, the dragon image is forced, and despite the valiant effort of chap. F one has difficulty shaking the suspicion that the apocalyptic scenario of Mordecai's dream was, at least in part, originally independent of the book of Esther. In addition, note that the order of decoding in chap. F conforms more closely to the events in the narrative than to the sequence within Mordecai's premonitory dream itself.

Esther F:6–8 displays the explicitly theological interpretation of the book that is characteristic of the Greek versions but contrasts markedly with the Hebrew recension. Verse 7 reflects an interpretation of the apparent plurality of the word *pūrîm* as an indication of the existence of two lots, one for Israel and one for the Gentiles, another innovation over against the MT. It is possible that v. 10 associates the two days of Purim with the two lots, though this is not certain. As in the case of 9:21–22 and 27, so here it is possible to understand the verse to mean that all Jews should observe *both* days, but it is not necessary to read it that way (see the commentary on 9:19). Whereas the MT of Esther ends with the greatness of Mordecai, prime minister of Persia and beloved protector of his fellow Jews (10:2–3), the LXX ends with a reiteration of the normativity and religious character of Purim (F:10). This probably reflects a later period in Jewish history, when the presence of a powerful intercessor in the Persian court was no longer an issue and the status of Purim had become a pressing question.

---

[241]See Levenson, *Creation*, 3–50.

2. Colophon (F:11) (Esther 11:1 in the Vulgate)

In the fourth year of the reign of Ptolemy and Cleopatra, Dositheus, who said he was a priest and a Levite, and Ptolemy his son, brought the fore-going letter of Purim, which they said was authentic and had been trans-lated by Lysimachus, son of Ptolemy, a member of the community of Jerusalem.

Esther F:11 is known as the colophon to the Greek Esther. Essentially a note appended to a manuscript by a copyist or a librarian attesting to its authenticity, the colophon is a familiar convention of the Hellenistic world. This one seems at first to hold out the promise of providing a secure date for the translation and thus a *terminus ad quem* for the earlier versions of the book of Esther as well. Unfortunately, the colophon to the Greek Esther proves unable to fulfill either promise. First, the identity of the Egyptian king mentioned is unclear, there having been several Ptolemies with wives named Cleopatra who reigned for four years or more. The dates suggested for the colophon thus range from 114–13, through 78–77, to 49–48 B.C.E.[242] The identity of "the foregoing letter of Purim" is also unknown, for we cannot be sure of the form of the Greek Esther to which this colophon was originally appended. One can speculate as to how Dositheus and his son determined that the document to which they attested was indeed "authentic" and what inauthentic variants competed with it, perhaps even in their own experience. But these points remain unknown as well. Dositheus's claim to be a priest and a Levite is intended further to reinforce the authenticity of the document he brought to Egypt. He is not a spurious priest, appointed by some Hellenistic king contrary to the rule of the Torah that a priest (*kōhēn*) must be a descendant of Aaron. Dositheus is, rather, from Aaron's tribe of Levi and thus a valid religious official.[243] The use of the term "letter (*epistolē*) of Purim" re-flects the Hebrew term *'iggeret* in 9:26 and 29 and provides the earliest evidence for the well-known Jewish interpretation of the term in those verses as referring to the book of Esther itself.[244] It is interesting, however, that the colophon seems to think that "Letter of Purim" is the name of what we have come to know as the book of Esther. When and why the book came to be known by Esther's name is another unsolved mystery.

---

[242]See Benno Jacob, "Das Buch Esther bei den LXX," *ZAW* 10 (1890): 278–79; Elias Bickerman, "The Colophon of the Greek Book of Esther," *JBL* 63 (1944): 339–62; rpt. in Moore, *Studies*, 529–52.

[243]Ralph Marcus, "Dositheus, Priest and Levite," *JBL* 64 (1945): 269–71.

[244]E.g., Targum Sheni to 9:26 and 29, in which *'iggeret* ("letter") is rendered as *měgiltā'* ("megillah," a name for the book of Esther).

INDEX OF ANCIENT SOURCES